BEFORE WE GO LIVE

Stephen Flavall is a leading strategy game streamer as "jorbs" on Twitch.tv, where he has a growing 100,000 follower community. He holds multiple world records in difficult strategy games, and currently concentrates on *Slay the Spire*. After a brief but successful career in poker, he rediscovered his love of storytelling. In a live feed, he plays some of the most difficult games in the world, sharing his joyful and engaging thought processes with his viewers, and using the impartial and widely appealing rule sets of gaming to find connection with people from all over the world. He also creates YouTube videos, where his channel has 60,000 followers. At the age of 12, he immigrated to the U.S. from New Zealand, and now lives in Seattle.

BEFORE WE GO LIVE

Navigating the abusive world of
online entertainment

by Stephen Flavall

 Spender Books

First published by Spender Books, 2023

spenderbooks.com

Cover artwork: @Zyalin_Art

PB ISBN: 9781739285906

e ISBN: 9781739285913

10 9 8 7 6 5 4 3 2 1

CONTENT WARNING

As a thirty-five-year-old entertainer, I value some amount of privacy, for myself and the people close to me. Several names in this book have been changed, and a few have been omitted. However, I also value being able to clearly and honestly communicate about important and sensitive elements of my life. I want to be an honest role model for my audience and a strong advocate and ally for my friends, and I want future content creators to be able to learn from my experiences and mistakes.

This book is my attempt to communicate about those sensitive elements via a medium which allows me to carefully review exactly what I say. Many of the topics covered are too serious or personal to talk about during a live show online. The story I have to tell is about people whom I love, and ways in which we have been taken advantage of, and I have needed a comfortable and controlled space to allow me to tell it in a way which is useful, evocative, and respectful of all of our boundaries.

Because of all this, some of the book is dark and troubling to read. Difficult subjects which were tangential have deliberately been sequestered in a segment of chapters toward the end of the book that contain little plot information relevant to the main story. Chapter Thirteen speaks about burnout through the coronavirus pandemic. Chapter Fourteen relates in detail a miscarried pregnancy a friend suffered, and her difficulty finding support in the predominantly male strategy gaming space she works in. Chapter Fifteen concerns mental illness and suicide. While I hope that you will read and empathize with these chapters, I also hope that you will find that the book is wholly readable and enjoyable should you choose to skip them.

The main story in this book would have been incomplete without a constant and thorough relating and examination of sexism, abuse (at work, but also in relationships and families), and manipulation, and these themes were impossible to contain within just a few chapters. You will find elements of them on most pages. It is my opinion that they are worth talking about, and this book is my attempt to do so.

This is for Hannah.
She'd like for you to read it, too.

NUMBERS

Sometimes I try to track all the numbers.

As of June 2022, I follow 492 people on Twitter, which is far too many people for me to actually care about, and am followed by 8,555, which is even worse. 60,000 people subscribe to my YouTube channel, and 109,000 follow my Twitch stream.

The numbers don't make much sense to me anymore. They are too large for me to understand. When I was starting out, I cared about smaller numbers. For a while I cared about paying rent: I made three dollars an hour; I made four; I made eight. After a year and a half of streaming full-time, I was finally making minimum wage. A couple of years after that, I was signed to a professional team and signing contracts to advertise products to my audience for $1,000 an hour.

I stopped trying to distinguish all my followers back when I had a few hundred. At the time, I figured I could meet and learn about five new people per day, if I really spent energy on it, but in the time it took me to do that, ten more would have followed my channel. Then it got really out of hand, and I started gaining hundreds of new followers every day. Nowadays there are people whom I know nothing about who have watched a thousand hours of my channel and tipped thousands of dollars to me.

My friend celebrates her three-millionth follower. A viewer announces their sixtieth consecutive month subscribed to my channel.

Today I am streaming *Slay the Spire*. I am constructing a deck of cards that I can play to protect myself and attack my enemies, and I am using it to ascend to the top of a fantasy Spire, battling enemies ranging from tiny lice to charismatic bandits to ritualistic cultists, and slay the Corrupt Heart which pumps blood into its walls from its peak. I have streamed 5,033 hours of this game and am the first person in the world to beat it while rotating through its characters at the highest difficulty seven, eight, nine, eleven, fourteen, fifteen, and sixteen times in a row. Today, after almost a month of play without losing, I am positioned to reach seventeen. One game usually takes me about ninety minutes to play, but in a high-stakes situation like this it can take more like three days. Three hours to get into my zone, four hours for the run itself—full of calculation and strategizing[1]—and then two days after to calm down again, to ease my shoulders back from their stressed and coiled hunch, and to be able to feel the ground under my hips again when I lie on my back. To convince my body to sleep for eight hours in a row. And then, if I've won, I'll start the process again to try for eighteen.

The stress isn't about the game. I have 2,422 viewers watching me right now, and when this run is posted to YouTube it will reach another twenty thousand. The viewers tend to compare me to three other prominent *Slay the Spire* players. Twelve people have suggested that I should have done something differently in the last five minutes. I have been told that I don't understand how to play some of the game's characters and that it's inappropriate for me to give opinions about them. I have been told that my voice is nice, and that it's annoying, and asked why it sounds the way it does. I've been told to dress differently, to play differently, to speak differently, to stop trying to be funny, to stop explaining my thoughts about the game, to stream at a different time. I've been

---

1   There are four *Slay the Spire* characters to master. Each has seventy-five cards to consider. There are 178 relics I might find, and sixty-four enemies I might fight, as I ascend a Spire's fifty-seven floors. My deck of thirty cards has 142,506 possible starting hands, and I have never piloted a deck quite like this one before.

told I shouldn't care about winning so much, and that I should care about winning more than I do, and that I should stop playing quick runs rotating through the characters and instead spend six hours per run on the same character for two months straight in order to prove that I'm actually good at the game. Thousands of people love me, but I also hear from those to whom I seem arrogant, naive, boring, slow, old, fat, awkward, insecure, and so on; some of them seem happy to share these opinions of me.

As I enter the final fight of the game, one enemy away from seventeen wins in a row, messages from my viewers get overwhelming. Dozens of viewers are suggesting strategies for the fight and telling me not to forget certain details, and I can't hear myself think. A moderator decides to set the channel to emote-only mode, so no one can send text messages anymore. With the click of a button, I see the community I've built—where I've spent ten thousand hours talking with my viewers about school and life and a pandemic and wars and charity and love—reduced to a flood of silly image spam.

In the end, I can't focus on the fight. I make a small mistake, and it's enough to make me lose. Maybe I would have lost anyway. Technically, I could go back and find out, but I don't care. Seventeen is not actually one of the numbers which matters to me. I care about trying my best for my viewers, but there are much more important goals than winning at this video game.

There are smaller numbers, and those are the most important to me. In my inbox, there are three emails from viewers crediting me with huge positive changes in their lives. There is one message on Twitter from an alcoholic asking me for money. There is one DM on Discord expressing suicidal ideation and requesting my help. There are five sponsored streams this week that I need to prepare for.

And there is one person I trust to make all of this approachable for me. Her name is Hannah, and she's been working with me for three years. She has passwords to six of my online accounts and access to a bank account which she uses to manage and pay my two other employees and a variety of contractors she hires on my behalf. She reads and responds to emails for me. But she's never been on my stream with me, and the vast majority of my viewers don't even know she exists.

This isn't a story about the big numbers. It's about the small ones that Hannah and I deal with while the stream is offline. It's about the unique, bizarre, and dangerous world the two of us have to navigate before I go live.

On this day, I have 3,581 notifications on Discord, almost all of which I ignore. As I end my stream, defeated by the Spire, I see that there is one from Hannah in the private server we use to organize everything that I put out into the world. I don't know if I'm about to be invited to fly to Los Angeles to meet a celebrity, or if she's found a contractor for art I'm trying to commission. Maybe a viewer has requested I sign a birthday card for their husband, or her ex has sent flowers to her house again. What I do know is that with this message, this single notification, the other numbers have already stopped mattering.

FADE2KARMA

To understand streaming, you will also need to understand the organizations that exist behind the scenes. The one I joined, back in 2018, was called Fade2Karma.

Fade2Karma, or F2K, had been founded in 2015, after a man named John missed a flight. The problem wasn't traffic, or misplacing his ticket, or getting lost on the way. He simply had a fear of flying and couldn't make himself get on the plane.

At the time, John was a professional *Hearthstone* player—a new thing for him, and for the world. Released in March 2014, *Hearthstone* was an online game heavily inspired by trading card games, but with no physical cards or trading. All your "cards" were collected in an online account, and you could play against people all over the world with any computer connected to *Hearthstone*'s online servers. It was a revolutionary and immediately successful idea. You no longer had to worry about cards getting damaged or lost—they were all kept safely in your account for you. Cards could have extremely complex effects, because to play them in the game, you didn't need to calculate anything—the online server could resolve everything for you. The cards could have beautiful animations and voice lines attached to them, and when you played games against other people, you didn't have to work to find an opponent at your level, or even shuffle your own deck.

John took to it naturally, earning $3,700 over his first year on the online tournament circuit and becoming an established face in the *Hearthstone* community. He had grown up collecting baseball cards and playing somewhat comparable strategy card games, like *Magic: The Gathering* and poker. *Hearthstone* was an exciting blend of familiar concepts he had already mastered, and soon he was holding his own against the best in the world. Eventually, he was even recruited to a professional team. With their support, he'd been on his way to his first in-person tournament, an event held at a live studio to be filmed and broadcast to fans around the world—that is, until the plane had left without him.

I'll interject here to say that whatever else I might think about John now, he is undeniably an impressive businessman and born leader. All evidence I've seen suggests strongly that he talks and schemes nonstop from the moment he wakes up until the moment he falls asleep. In typical John fashion, he took this setback—the missed flight—and turned it into an opportunity. Instead of being a professional player himself, he left his team to found Fade2Karma, a brand-new professional *Hearthstone* team.

The selling point was simple: He framed his failure to attend the tournament as a failure of the team which had recruited him to properly provide for him, and claimed that F2K was going to treat its players "right." F2K would put goodness out into the world, and karma, he claimed, would do the rest. F2K's business model was similarly simple: They signed players whom they thought would succeed at *Hearthstone*, coached them, and paid for them to travel to tournaments, receiving a cut of any winnings the players earned in return.

The team grew slowly but successfully, eventually expanding its goals. Many successful *Hearthstone* players were streaming their gameplay on services like Twitch and could reach live audiences of hundreds or thousands of people. It quickly became clear that the money available in the form of donations and subscriptions from the audience of a streamer or content creator—someone who wasn't just playing *Hearthstone* but was also entertaining viewers at the same time—was far more significant than the prize money available at tournaments. So F2K stopped prioritizing tournaments and started offering salaries based on the number of hours viewers spent watching players' channels, then taking commission for finding them advertising contracts with companies in the online space.

Three years later, in 2018, I found that I was, myself, in need of a team like F2K. After a short and lucrative career in online poker, I had found my way to streaming. I'd started streaming full-time in 2016, broadcasting myself playing complex strategy video games with incredibly nerdy titles like *XCOM: Enemy Unknown* and *Faster Than Light*, which appealed to small communities of die-hard fans. I'd tackle one and establish mastery of it, winning viewers from its community, and then move on to challenge myself with the next. *Slay the Spire*, a single-player card game not entirely unlike *Hearthstone*, had caught my fancy, and then it had completely exploded in popularity, taking my channel up along with it. Suddenly, a couple thousand people were watching my channel every day instead of the couple hundred I had gotten used to.

If you've watched online videos on sites like YouTube, you might be familiar with the way content creators advertise products. A common example is a sixty-second shout-out which the creator inserts into their video, introduced with something like, "But before we get to that, I want to take a moment to thank our sponsor for making this video possible." Note that the sponsor probably did not make the video possible in any way; someone getting millions of views on YouTube is already making a living wage off YouTube's advertising revenue share, and the sponsor provided absolutely no labor toward writing the script or otherwise creating the video. At most, they might provide some graphical assets and talking points for the sponsored segment. What the sponsor *did* do was send the person who made the video, or their team or agent, an email saying that they'd pay a few thousand dollars for a product placement. These deals can be concluded fairly easily with a few short emails and the addition of a signature to an online document.

Unfortunately, there is no guarantee that the businesses reaching out to arrange these advertising contracts are desirable, ethical, or offering a fair payment. Because of this, it can be useful to join an org—a team like F2K, which is made up of a large number of streamers (in the forty to eighty range, in F2K's case) and which uses that fact to leverage collective bargaining power, hire staff who understand the space, and ideally find its streamers better deals for better money and from better companies. A great team might even be able to help your channel grow by throwing its brand behind it.

John and his staff flagged my channel, noting its successful growth and my mastery of the sorts of strategy games the team was known for, and John reached out to me in December 2018. Cold-calling in this industry is a necessity, and I think the way that John messaged me says a lot about F2K and why they were successful. The usual type of cold call I receive is clearly based on a template and shows up in my email. While it might try to sound impressive and profitable, it typically does not hint at humanity at almost any point. Meanwhile, I think John's message to me on Discord—a more personal medium than email, where I chat with friends and viewers—is the best I've ever seen:

> "Hey Stephen, my name is John I'm the CEO of F2K, Esports and stream team, I was watching your stream yesterday for a bunch and I really like the vibes and the content, you already got me with the too many kooks title tbh. Also your gaming history is quite interesting to me since it is very similar to mine. Anyways, I really liked what I saw and would to have a chat at some point to see if it might make sense to work together. Keep up the good work! Cheers, John"

As I would come to learn, everything about this message exuded John. The missing words because he was too busy and excited and frantic to notice the errors. The familiarity and affection. The invitation to do something that would be fun because it was with him, even if it didn't end up being what you'd wanted. The message sounded less like a team trying to contract me and more like someone reaching out in the hopes of making a new friend. In an age full of cold calls—not just in business, but in online dating and other aspects of life as well—I think this one is instructive.

No one gives you a "promotion" in streaming. You go from streaming in front of five viewers to five hundred or five thousand viewers with no change in your job title. Receiving an offer from a legitimate streaming team is one of a very few milestones that you can point to as a sign that you're really getting somewhere. Even nowadays, after finishing two and a half years with F2K and having significantly grown my channel, I would be excited to respond to a message like this from someone like John. Back then, it was exhilarating.

A week later, I jumped on a call with John. We chatted for an hour, getting to know each other a bit. We connected effortlessly—he'd quit teaching history around the same time I'd dropped out of the classics program at my university, and we easily bonded over our passion for transforming a deep analysis of the past into mastery of analytical games in the present. After the call, he presented me with a contract, offering $1,000 or so per month in exchange for advertising F2K and its partners on my channel (scaling with the number of viewers I reached and hours I streamed) as well as some other contributions to F2K's brand, like displaying their logo on my social media accounts. F2K would also try to bring me personal advertising contracts from businesses that I didn't feel I could have reached on my own, taking a fairly small commission for doing so. I considered and negotiated for a couple of weeks, then signed an updated contract on December 31, 2018. Suddenly a career which had started as a hobby had put me on a professional team.

***

Charity work had always been one of my cornerstones as a content creator. For several years, I'd spent twenty-four sleepless hours every Christmas Day running a stream in which all of my revenue was sent directly to charity. I still believe—despite all contrary evidence—that humans are basically good and just need a bit of help sometimes, so I had begun raising money to fund tutors for at-risk kids, clean water for struggling communities, suicide hotlines, and so on.

When I joined F2K, I'd been planning a Valentine's Day charity stream. I tried to run charity streams on days when people might be in need of comfort: Christmas, Thanksgiving, Valentine's Day. The noble ideal was that someone who'd just been dumped or couldn't get home to be with family could hang out with us for the day and do something good. (In actual practice, sometimes a viewer might ignore the love of their life all day on a holiday because they wanted to watch me play a video game and make bad jokes about capitalism.[2] But I was trying to do good, and I think overall these streams achieved that.)

I mentioned the Valentine's Day stream to John, who then mentioned it to the staff. The next day, I met Hannah. As F2K's Chief of Operations at the time, she took over, quickly putting together an awesome charity event. I'd been expecting a little bit of support for the stream—maybe a graphic to hype it up and a

---

2   For most of my streaming career, I dated a woman who had met me before I was a streamer, and who had to learn to put up with me choosing to be busy on all of these days. I would be remiss not to mention how difficult that was for her, as well.

shout-out on the team's social media accounts. Instead, Hannah made me the main attraction of a team-wide charity event, with several other streamers joining in to raise money and a lot of general hype from F2K. This was cool! The event broke my previous record for money raised in a day on my channel, and it allowed me to collaborate with some new faces from the team. Right away, F2K felt like a happening place to be, like it was really trying to do some good in the world.

The only thing that I didn't love about the event was that Hannah wasn't around to see it succeed. After pulling a massive charity drive together for me, she'd left the company under unclear circumstances a week before it occurred. Already she was the most impressive person I'd ever met on the backend of esports, but she'd left the company after only a month of us working together.

***

If you are a human being, you've been exposed to gender expectations throughout your life. Men are strong; women are supportive—those types of messages. When you take a bunch of people who believe and act on these messages and put them on a team together, particularly in a traditionally male-dominated space like gaming, gender is bound to have an effect on the team's dynamics. Ideally, you'd hope that adult professionals would grow out of this, but I haven't yet seen much evidence to support that. And when fifteen of those people are men and one of them is a woman, it's easy to predict that issues related to gender might come up.

Hannah grew up gaming. She was a *World of Warcraft* girl; as of the publication of this book, she still plays quite seriously with friends. She'd dated gamers, befriended gamers—almost all male. She used to play team games with her microphone off and an androgynous name so that she'd be treated as "one of the guys." But gamers have often treated her like she's lesser, because she's a woman, and no matter what she has done, it has never been enough.

Hannah is incredibly good at what she does but "lacks confidence"—or at least that is what someone else might say about her. She grew up being told not to talk over others, so in online group voice calls, especially over long distances when latency means noticeable wait-times before you can be confident that nobody else is speaking, she mostly doesn't say anything. One time I was in a call with her and a potential collaborator, and she didn't realize that her microphone had been muted until after the hour-long call was over. She'd said very little, I'd assumed she was happy just taking notes, and when she did say something, it had seemed normal to her that the other people on the call didn't react to it at all. That was on a call with me and one other woman. You can maybe imagine how this dynamic is increased when the calls are bigger and louder and include more and more boisterous men beaming about how they think they're inventing the next big thing online.

Hannah had also been one of F2K's foundational employees. She'd spent four years growing the org from a small *Hearthstone* esports team into a large online content creator network, working unhealthily long hours for little pay. And she'd loved it! When I joined, she was officially the team's Chief of Operations, but her real role was a little more complicated. She didn't like overseeing calls with sponsors—not her thing—and John didn't like managing backend stuff—not his thing—so they'd settled into traditional gender roles. She kept things comfy at home, providing emotional support and guidance when he needed it, and he took charge of the public-facing elements of the company.

To me there was nothing particularly unjust about this arrangement. What happened next, however, was bad.

As F2K grew, John found himself wearing more and more hats, overwhelmed with more and more work. As was Hannah, of course. And in early 2019, shortly after I joined the team, he decided that he needed a public-facing Chief of Operations. He checked in with Hannah and asked if it would be okay for him to bring someone else in to do the public facing COO work.

Hannah had been open to the possibility, but she didn't trust that the candidate John had in mind knew what he was doing—he had far less experience than her—and she wasn't signed off on sharing the COO responsibilities in general. But another message we're told about gender is that men are expected to make decisions and women are expected to deal with it, so the next day John announced that F2K had a new COO and introduced us to Joe—a longtime friend of his who used to watch him when he streamed his *Hearthstone* games way back in the day. John had technically granted Hannah's request not to share the role, in the cruelest way possible. She had been demoted, and Joe was now her boss.

Hannah was also pregnant at the time, and while you might reasonably expect that the world should be structured otherwise, the reality was that a pregnant employee at F2K did not have easy access to healthcare or other supports. So, she left the team on bad terms and found employment in a more traditional job.

I'd gotten the sense that Hannah's leaving the team was deeply personal and that I shouldn't ask about it—which was at most half true—but I also knew that she was the most impressive person I'd worked with in my time as a content creator. She'd thrown together a massive charity event for me out of nowhere, on an extremely small budget. In one month of working together, she'd worked out my main traits as a content creator, my motivations, and the ways I wanted to be sponsored and promoted. She was kind and listened, and if you shut up and let her talk, she had nothing but positive and insightful things to say. She had more experience talking with sponsors and creators in esports than almost anyone else in the world, and her command of these conversations was obvious. At the time that she left, I'd felt that getting to work with Hannah had been a quarter or a third of the sum value I was getting out of my contract with F2K, so I checked with John that it would be okay and then reached out to ask her if she'd work for me directly.

Hannah can still remember that day. She tells me that she read my message in bed, then jumped out of bed and read it two or three more times. I had said that I'd been impressed by her when we worked together, and she was racking her brain trying to remember what she'd done to seem so impressive. (To this day, Hannah does not understand how impressive she is.) She says: "It was a good day. The first person I told was my mom."

Hannah has been working for me ever since. It took me a couple of years to work out how to make her accept more than $30 per hour, but I'm proud to say that I've finally got her taking commission. She pays herself out of our business account, and sometimes I've had to work pretty hard to convince her to take any money at all. In my view, her belief that the tremendous amount of availability, emotional labor, and expertise that she provides isn't worth paying for is a gigantic red flag about the space that she's worked in and depended on over the course of her life.

HANNAH

Hannah's parents both immigrated to the United States from South Korea, from a deep and poor countryside along the mountains called Gapyeong. Her father had a traumatic and tumultuous childhood, characterized by abandonment by his own parents, abuse from his relatives, and a level of poverty which forced him to fish rotten vegetables out of the trash and steal food from stalls so he wouldn't starve to death. She never heard any of those stories about his childhood from him, though; they were always recounted by her mother, or her aunts. As an adult, Hannah forgave him for years of abuse toward herself and her mother during her childhood, reasoning that when a child grows up the way he did, they can't survive it without scars. They can't be whole again—but they can be better, and he did get better with age.

When he'd moved to America, he was an eighteen-year-old in classes for fifteen-year-olds, because his English was almost nonexistent. His family situation remained incredibly dysfunctional, but in America, he didn't have to starve. In America, he could build a better life with easier opportunities, which would never have been open to someone like him with no education or family reputation in Korea. He started opening businesses in inner-city St. Louis: a convenience store, a Chinese fast-food restaurant, a beauty supply store. This last was the most successful and long-standing.

Hannah has always known her father to have an abrasive personality, not caring what others think about him as long as he gets what he wants. To this day, he prides himself on being able to negotiate anything into his favor, often using the language barrier between himself and native English speakers to his advantage. He'd realized early on that the less people understood him, the better chance he had for them to give up and just give him what he wanted. His obstinate nature made him an incredibly rugged but efficient businessman. During Hannah's childhood, both of her parents worked twelve-hour days, seven days a week, in the small businesses they created. She spent the weekends there with her little brother, so they could keep an eye on the kids while they weren't in school or daycare.

Throughout Hannah's life, her father always told her that he wanted her and her brother to take over the family business. Growing up with that in mind, no matter how many jobs she'd had in between, if she ever needed work, she could find it at the beauty supply store. Her parents would put her straight back into the shop and pay her cash.

When Hannah was twenty-four years old, she had just come back home from working in New Jersey for a wholesaler. Her boss had gone into a fit of rage over a small mistake in an invoice—screaming at the top of his lungs and throwing and kicking the space heater she had because he never turned on the heat in winter—and she had decided it was time to quit and make her way back home. Her parents let her back into the store at $10 an hour. They had opened a second location and needed help in the main store anyway, so it worked out nicely.

After two years, they put Hannah into the management position at the main store. She tracked revenues, made coupons to give out to customers, and raised sales by 30% in three months. The secondary store was run by one of her dad's close friends, but it was failing. The other manager kept the doors locked, so Hannah's father had installed a bell at the door. Many customers failed to see the bell—who would think a retail store would have a bell you had to ring to gain access? Hannah also found her incredibly rude; it was clear that she didn't care about the customers and didn't even want to be there. Needless to say, the business started losing customers until it became full days open-to-close with no customers walking through the locked door. So, Hannah's father shut it down and merged all the merchandise back to the main store, demoting Hannah to assistant manager because he didn't fully believe she was mature enough to run the main store as manager, especially if he had to bring the manager from the second shop into the main one. None of Hannah's achievements were even mentioned or considered in his decision.

Hannah tried to accept it gracefully, so she wouldn't burden her parents with tantrums or petty anger, but she *was* angry, and felt betrayed by her own flesh and blood.

***

At the time, she was playing *World of Warcraft* casually. She'd joined a guild and gotten very close to the people in it, playing long hours of the game together on the Internet. The guild leader, Sam, always bragged about being the co-founder of an esports team called Good Gaming, and said that another co-founder was out getting investors.

Shortly after Hannah's demotion at the store, Sam told her that Good Gaming had found an investor and that they needed volunteers. They were building an online tournament platform for all sorts of games—putting together online events like the *Hearthstone* tournaments that John had played in. The investor was willing to put in money for prize pools to kick off the branding and make it a worldwide hub for online competition. Hannah said she would take any work he had to offer her.

She started her first day at Good Gaming as a volunteer tournament admin. She wasn't being paid, but she decided that if she offered her work in good faith and excelled to the point that they needed her, they would eventually offer some compensation. And so she became the best tournament admin she could be, and started helping to organize the tournaments as well.

After a couple of months, Sam told her he wanted to have a call with her, dragged her into a chatroom on Discord, and told her that the company would like to hire her at $1,000 per month. She took it, graciously thanking him a million times. She let her parents know that her friend had given her an online job and quit the store. They asked a hundred questions about what kind of job it was, but when she tried explaining an Internet job to a pair of people who had grown up without a working toilet, she found it was almost impossible. After an hour of her trying to explain it, her dad waved his hand and said, "As long as it's a real job and not a scam, I trust you." That's how they left it.

Days at Good Gaming had their highs and lows. The investor was a man in his sixties or seventies named Dale. He had a right-hand man, Mike, whom Hannah characterizes as an "Igor type." Together they felt like something out of a TV show.[3] Hannah felt that Dale ruled by fear, constantly threatening people that they would be out of their job if they didn't do something correctly, to the point that the threat started to lose meaning and she felt like she was listening to the ramblings of a senile old man. "Yes, yes, Dale. I understand. You'll have what you need by end of day, today," she would say, and he would grumble a "thank you," and she could imagine him sitting back in an old leather office chair, puffing on a cigar, satisfied that he had gotten his way again and successfully scared an employee into submission. His daily dose of feeling like he was king, with her as his groveling peasant.

By the time she had worked there for a year, she'd learned a lot of new skills. If there was jargon she didn't understand, Google

---

3   I find repeatedly that the online space fails to set boundaries on behavior, resulting in humans resembling absurdist caricatures of the worst possible types.

was her best friend. There wasn't anything Google couldn't teach her and that she couldn't replicate and do. The platform was finally working on the front end, but navigating the backend was like sifting through duct tape and spit. There were two developers, Alex and Don. Don was chief technology officer, and it was incredibly apparent that he used his position to his favor by bragging that he could get Dale to agree to anything while he, himself, used Google to learn how to develop things as demands were made. What would take a normal developer a day to code would take him a week. Alex was the only true developer, and he worked like a dog, delegated whatever tasks Don couldn't find the code for on Google or YouTube. This was how Good Gaming's tournament platform was built, brick by brick, out of papier-mâché, newspaper strips, Scotch tape, and Alex's 100+ hours a week, always slaving and rarely sleeping.

***

Hannah's job was to schedule the tournaments, and at the time, *Hearthstone* was the most important game to run tournaments for to grow the platform. Blizzard, the company who made the game, was approving sanctioned tournaments to anyone who applied to run one and let them know the tournament schedule ahead of time. These sanctioned tournaments then fed into big worldwide tournaments that Blizzard held every season, inviting the players who'd won the most points. Hannah communicated with Blizzard employees to organize these tournaments, made sure points would be reported on time for the winners, and made sure the tournaments would be approved and advertised on Blizzard's tournament schedule website. She was able to secure Good Gaming's position as a regular tournament platform for the game. Dale praised her: She had done it! She had made the old man happy. Everyone was happy. They were official and could start rolling out tournaments.

They started running two or three tournaments a week, aimed at North American time zones. They were successful and started receiving more and more signups. Hannah controlled the admin work through the backend and the Discord servers they had set up. She became extremely meticulous because everything was so time sensitive. Announcements had to be exactly on time, tournaments had to be exactly on time. If a co-worker or competitor had a question, she dropped everything and tried to answer it within a minute of it being asked. If there was one thing she wanted people to remember about Good Gaming tournaments, it was that the tournament administration was fantastic—a platform glitch here and there would easily be forgotten. That's how she tried to make up for their dodgy system: great customer service.

***

Dale saw their progress and was ecstatic. He wanted more investment and more tournaments. Not just in North America—Europe too! Two or three tournaments a week quickly became ten. Then fourteen, two per day. Hannah was managing all of these tournaments, by herself, still at $1,000 a month, for a massive online tournament platform running tournaments for a game which was taking the world by storm. And she was succeeding, but she was starting to run out of steam. Then Dale announced that he had brought in an esports team called F2K to consult, help "make our tournaments better," and provide more admins. Sam, Don, Alex, and Hannah were all confused. Who was F2K? Why did Dale think the tournaments should be better? And that's how she met John.

John introduced himself as the CEO of F2K and said he would be coming into Good Gaming as the chief of operations. He'd been in the industry the longest of any of them. He understood the competitive space and strongly believed that *Hearthstone* would be what Good Gaming needed to focus on to get more organic website visits and more tournament players signing up autonomously to its platform.

The first working experience Hannah had with him was when Good Gaming ran a 2v2 *Call of Duty* tournament. The platform broke at the beginning of the tournament, and John made a decision to use the "pen and paper" method on the brackets to keep the tournament moving. She was in awe, seeing someone who was so fast with decisions and who understood exactly what to do to defuse a problem which could have easily meant a complete failure of the tournament. He handled the staff like an orchestra, telling them what they had to do and when, and they followed like instruments as he conducted.

She found him charismatic, with a charming stutter when he got excited, and down-to-earth. She wasn't used to his German accent, and it took her quite a long time before she could understand what he was saying without asking him to repeat himself. He wasn't someone who was just your boss—he was also your friend. He brought in Gareth, Mat, and Aleks from F2K to work as admins under Hannah, still the only woman at the company, and he encouraged her to continue doing an excellent job. By his recommendation, she was promoted from tournament admin to tournament director, and the department was hers to control. It was the first time she felt someone actually gave her a chance to take control of something in her own way and trusted her to do it.

Her loyalty to John grew because he followed through with his promises. When he mentioned promotion, she got it. When he found out she was getting paid $1,000 a month for working over sixty hours a week, he exclaimed that it was the most ridiculous thing he'd ever heard and organized a raise to $1,500. She felt like she was finally being taken care of by someone who could see her worth—who didn't just tell her that she was valuable, but actually showed her that she was.

Hannah will tell you that she is a simple person, although I tend to think she underestimates herself. Her life's motto of being good to others begins by always giving the benefit of the doubt to someone, and she won't stop trusting and respecting them unless they demonstrate a consistent pattern of cruelty and manipulation. Trusting people right off the bat had always been a weakness of hers, and John didn't give her any reasons to not trust him.

As Good Gaming began to get bigger investors—including a major venture capitalist—their tournaments expanded from North America and Europe to Asia as well. Hannah hired Korean translators and woke up at 2 a.m. to be able to oversee the tournament beginnings, helping until they all died down enough for her to slide back into bed and catch a few more hours of sleep before her actual full work day began. She was getting stretched thin, and pleaded to John that considering the amount she was working, she should be compensated more. He came back with another raise to $2,000 a month, and that kept her happy enough to continue with her grueling schedule.[4]

She says, thinking back now, that she would do it all over again. It was the happiest time of her life. She had moved to Alabama at the time to live with her cousin. Her cousin was pregnant and wanted to have family nearby, but she'd had to move to Alabama with her husband when he was transferred there for his job. Hannah says it's crazy to think about how she

---

4   Sanity check for readers: Yes, she absolutely should have been getting paid at least three or four times this much.

had the energy to work sixteen- to eighteen-hour days and still find time to cook dinner for her own boyfriend, Jake; her cousin; and her cousin's son and husband. In Korean culture, pregnancy is a big deal. A pregnant mother must always be fed good food, and Hannah took that philosophy to heart when she moved in. Despite never having an "off" period in her day, Hannah took comfort in feeling needed not only at her job, but also by her family.

During this time, Hannah took a rare weekend off to visit a close friend in Missouri whose baby had been born prematurely. In her friend's backyard, Hannah got a phone call from John to tell her that Good Gaming's venture capital investor had decided to focus on profiting from micro-transactions in *Minecraft*, and was shutting down the tournament department. She remembers pacing back and forth, slapping off mosquitoes, feeling her heart pounding out of her chest because she didn't know what she would do for income. The entire tournament department was sitting in a Discord call, listening to John fire them all.

Then John called out her name and told her he wanted to talk to her after the call. He called her directly, and asked her if she wanted to come work for F2K. Her heart was pounding for another reason now.

"Are you telling me that I never have to deal with Dale's incessant need to threaten us every day that one of us will get fired, or listen to Mike's drunken ramblings as he shamelessly grabs another beer out of his fridge during company meetings?" The guy who had taken care of her the entire time she was in Good Gaming was offering her a job. It was difficult for her to talk; all she can remember saying was "thank you," over and over again. She was relieved that she wouldn't have to go through the hard process of putting in applications for a job in Alabama, and relieved that someone thought she was good enough to hire her after seeing her work ethic.

She remembers asking him, "But what exactly would I do in F2K?" She knew F2K didn't have a tournament department.

He told her that she could start off as his personal assistant; he needed one. Once she'd learned how the company worked, they'd find other things for her to do. She could tell he was smiling and pleased that he had just hired her on the spot. He said he'd never met anyone who could work like her and probably never would again, so he needed her at F2K.

She pledged her work soul to John. He told her that she'd start when she got back. He put her on a call with Gareth, Mat, and Aleks, and they all congratulated her and welcomed her into F2K. They had all told him to hire her, that it was a no-brainer that he should.

She was elated. She told Jake about it later, and he was talking her up about how she was so valuable and how if someone couldn't see that about her, they were crazy. She thought he was the one who was crazy for saying that. She thought she was only as good as her work, and that she had a lot of improvements to make.

The idea that she had spearheaded the ascent of an international tournament organization in a brand-new field, and how impressive that was, didn't really register for Hannah. She had been told that she wasn't good enough by too many people for too long. It's an experience which resonates with many women I talk to about streaming.

In Hannah's mind, she was about to go into a job she had no clue about, and she could feel anxiety eating her up. But she kept that to herself. She silently pep-talked herself on the six-hour drive back to Alabama, vowing that she would do her best to become an asset that F2K couldn't get rid of.

On her first day of work for F2K, Hannah woke up at four in the morning. She was aware that everyone else in the company was from Europe and was seven hours ahead of her. She wasn't going to make them put any of their work on hold just because she was behind; she figured she could easily adjust her schedule to fit theirs. John hopped on a call with her, and they started talking about what he had going on for him on a day-to-day basis. She realized there was too much disorganization—nothing with an actual schedule that he could look at—so she brought up a Google Sheet and made him a scheduled task list. She reminded him about things throughout the day, and he called her often to update her on his conversations with people.

As she became more acclimated to F2K, she began to learn about the streamers on the team, sometimes getting thrown into random calls with them so John could show her off as the newbie in the company and tell them she was his assistant. It was hard for her to absorb it all. Streamers are low-level celebrities of the Internet, and she was nervous every time she went into a new call with someone, wanting to make the best possible first impressions. She tried to be extremely professional.

If I could time travel, I would go back in time to tell past Hannah that nobody else had a clue what was going on either. The entire concept of streaming was brand new, and she was learning a lot faster than the rest of them. And then I would go to a corner store I remember fondly in Italy and get pizza.

She learned over time that John had a strange method of talking to the team. He was never precise with details; it was always a one-liner with a maximum of ten words that everyone on the team needed to decipher.[5] He also never came out with the

5   I always assumed John just communicated strangely, but upon inspec-
     tion this feels like it was a deliberate attempt at Law 3 of *The 48 Laws
     of Power*: "Conceal Your Intentions." One of the ways I could tell I was
     getting close to John was when he started telling me about the books

point first: He'd always "ping" everyone with "Anyone around?" Nobody ever answered him faster than Hannah. She'd always been fast, and she wanted to become the person he would always lean on first. She felt like she owed him as much for bringing her in. Her way of thinking was heavily influenced by Korean culture and completely different from the others. In Korea, you never left work first—you only left when the boss went home. She'd learned that working at her parents' store. She adopted it within F2K because she respected John.

John was amused that he could hand her any task, and she wouldn't complain. She told him once, "It wouldn't be fun if it were easy." They referred back to this anecdote often, as he handed her things to do that she had never seen before. This became even more frequent when he introduced her to Dan, the business developer. She was going to help Dan with everything and anything he needed. John told Dan she had experience in sales.

**

Meeting Dan, Hannah's first impression was that he seemed an alright guy. He was incredibly friendly while talking to John before focusing on her. Then he asked her, "What's your background? What school did you go to?"

Hannah was a high school dropout. She had moved out of her house the moment she turned eighteen, after her dad had hit her in the head with a three-inch-thick geology book because a

---

he'd read to learn how to manipulate the people around him, with that one being a focal point, but they all seemed so absurd that I couldn't make myself believe he was being serious. I eventually dismissed him by telling him he should just use whatever he was learning to make me money, which felt like an appropriately crass attempt to reinforce professional boundaries at the time, but was disgustingly cavalier in retrospect.

friend had spilled soda on their wood floors. Her dad later told her that there was something different about the way she'd looked at him that day. He wasn't surprised when he found out a week later that she wasn't coming back home. She was tired of going to the hospital for made-up reasons, like that she "fell down some stairs," or hit a car door precisely on her left jaw and dislocated it. She was tired of telling her high school tennis coach that she ran into a light post when asked why she had a bruise on her cheek. She was tired of giving excuses that protected someone who was meant to protect her and didn't do it properly. But despite his giving her hell, she loved her father as much as she despised him. More than anything, she loved her family.

At age fifteen, she had told her mother that it was okay if she left her dad—Hannah would look after her younger brother, and they'd be okay. But she'd seen Korean families ruin each other's reputations with gossip, and calling him out publicly wasn't something she was willing to do. Her solution was to drop out the day she turned eighteen, leave a note for her parents, and disappear for half a year before she contacted them again. She lived on pennies, she took a lot of part-time jobs, and she was starving to the point of eating cereal with water, but she was happy. She travelled in small steps from Florida to New England, she experienced as much as she could, and she always believed that one day she'd work herself up to a position where she'd make enough of a living to never feel that gnawing pain in her stomach again. She could gain a reputation where people would respect her without having to ask her what college she came out of. She'd gain her father's respect.

But how do you summarize that for someone who is asking you about your educational background? How can you let someone summarize who you are—how professional or how experienced you are in the things you do—by simply telling them you were a high school dropout? Dan didn't care about her story. Hannah told him she had no college background, and she could almost feel the roll of his eyes through the Skype call. It became a thing later on. Dan would tell John that her ideas weren't good enough because she'd never gotten a degree. He'd claim he had more credibility because he graduated from some prestigious college that also gave degrees to a bunch of NFL players.

Dan never ended up finding a real sponsor for F2K. In fact, he siphoned the money from F2K into failed marketing ploys and making them do giveaways for sponsors for a couple hundred dollars of their own money. Meanwhile, Hannah tried to tell him that there were better ways to advertise through the streamers that could become more profitable for the team. She told me: "Why not stop sending a hundred emails a day to companies that are non-endemic and have not an ounce of an idea how this space works and focus more on individual activations, or go for brands that make the best sense for our streamers? Why not sell them on their viewership and minutes watched metrics, which are real numbers that could leverage a sale?" In 2017, she was trying to convince F2K to adopt what are now considered standard, successful industry practices.

But no, Hannah's opinions were dismissed as unusable, seemingly just because she had the wrong background. John would assure her that he didn't believe college education to be the measure of someone's ability or intelligence, but also say that he didn't want to undermine Dan's authority in his own department. So only John heard Hannah's ideas. And a couple of years later, when John demoted her, making someone else COO in her place, she left F2K and got a job at a warehouse, updating inventory. If I had joined the team a month later than I did, I might never have known she existed.

THE BEST SLAY THE SPIRE PLAYER
IN THE WORLD

Istarted playing games on the floor of my maternal grandfather's office when I was an infant. While my parents were at work, he'd sit at his desk and read some book, and I would sit on the floor and play board games by myself. I realized ten years later that he was reading the Bible the entire time, and it sort of made sense. He was religious, but he wasn't a huge fan of the church, and he was about as far away from evangelical as it's possible for someone to be, so he never told me anything about God or the Bible. But there I was on the floor while he was reading it, and so, by proximity, games became religious, spiritual, and contemplative for me. I learned chess notation at the same time that I learned to read.

I learned storytelling, too. My mother would write stories for me and leave them taped to the outside of her bedroom door, so every morning I'd wake up to personalized children's stories about me and my friends going on wondrous mini-golf adventures and the like. My father's side of the family was religious, full of Bible stories and kindness, and my mother's side was pedagogical, full of teachers and university professors and analysts. Her brother, my uncle, used to play *X-COM: UFO Defense*[6] on his computer and tell me stories about the characters in it and explain the strategies he was using and the concerns he had while he played, and I would sit behind him, enraptured. When I was eight, and we

---

6   The first of the franchise of games which would launch my streaming
     career, a little over twenty years later.

were both staying with my grandparents, I would carefully crack his door open to ask if he was sleeping. "Well, I'm not anymore!" he would respond, laughing, and roll out of bed to turn his computer on. He took me and my siblings camping (in sleeping bags in the backyard) and kept us awake for hours, telling us stories about the stars and summarizing tales from mythology and religion.

My dad worked with computers and had a job for a while building graphics and statistics for broadcasts of New Zealand cricket matches, and my mother was working on her economics PhD and taught me how to calculate and interpret standard deviations when I was ten. If you wanted to raise a strategy gamer in the nineties, you'd be hard-pressed to create conditions this perfect on purpose.

I grew up wanting to be a teacher like my grandmother, or a computer programmer like my dad. I didn't understand what my mother—an economist—did and assumed it was way too difficult for me to manage. The only professional gamers I knew of were unapproachable gods in the pages of my Bible, a hefty paperback containing *500 Grandmaster Games of Chess*. I never imagined that twenty-five years later, I'd be playing chess online in front of thousands of people with Peter Svidler, eight-time Russian National champion, coaching me and talking me through the positions we reached.

I vividly remember the first time I caught my mother "lying" to me. I had been absent-mindedly reading a paper she had left out on the dining room table which argued that the government should make any road improvement which was expected to reduce annual deaths of motorists by more than [some number] per [some amount of dollars]. I went to school the next day and explained to my friends that it was possible to calculate the monetary value of a human life. One expressed interest and asked, in the way an eight-year-old would, what it was. I had forgotten the exact number—I think the hypothetical language of the paper confused me and I didn't really understand if it were a "true" number or just an idea, plus I didn't really understand what numbers with that many zeroes meant yet—so I went home that night and looked for the paper.

When I couldn't find it, I asked my mother what the value of a human life was, and she told me it was priceless. I followed up by asking what the dollar value was, though, and she told me you couldn't place a dollar value on human life. I felt my world shatter; I thought my mother was lying to me.

Years later, looking back, I can see my misunderstanding— the point of the paper wasn't that spending more money than that was bad because a human life wasn't worth it; it was that spending more money than that was bad because the money could save more lives if spent elsewhere—but as a child I didn't get that yet.

I was scolded at my own birthday party that year. For dinner, we were served plates of our own food, with lollies and other sweet things put communally in the middle of the table for us to grab as we wanted, and I told everyone that the optimal strategy was for us to eat as much of the food in the middle as we could before it ran out, and only then eat from our own plates, in order to maximize the amount of delicious food we could get. My mother attempted to explain to me that that was selfish, but I didn't really get it. The strategy games I had been playing were selfish—they were about what you should do to make yourself win—and I didn't understand why I shouldn't act like I was playing a strategy game in the rest of my life. Plus, I'd told everyone else the best strategy, instead of keeping it to myself. Wasn't that the opposite of being selfish? I've met a lot of otherwise smart people who never worked the answer to that question out.

When I was twelve, my dad hit the top of his career ladder in New Zealand, and was scouted by software companies in the United States. And so my main childhood trauma was an international move and its aftermath, when I was suddenly going through puberty in another country with no extended family and no friends.

At university, I fell into poker. A grad student got drunk with me during a quarter I spent in Rome and told me I'd be good at it. I installed the PokerStars client on my laptop and spent a few of the evenings in Rome entering free tournaments online. After a week of learning, I won five dollars by placing in the top ten of a free 6,000-person tournament, and over the next few years, I turned those five dollars into a couple hundred thousand, without ever actually making a deposit on the site. I eventually dropped out of university—I was making more than my professors already, and my goal had been to work for another ten years to become one of them—and spent some time traveling the world, sitting down every now and then in a furnished room the size of a large closet in some exotic city to log in and spend the evening making some money.

I eventually got toward the top of the online poker ecosystem and hired a coach to help give me confidence and perspective to compete against the absolute best. He got me into the habit of recording myself playing for an hour while I vocalized my thoughts and reasons for doing what I was doing, and then he'd have me go back to review what I'd said after I was done playing.

I was entranced again. I was doing what my uncle had done for me as a kid, except I was doing it for myself. It was useful for learning, but even more so, it was useful for showing to other people. I started offering coaching myself and making videos of my play, which I shared publicly online. This was very unusual at this time in poker. Poker is a competitive game where having a strategic advantage which your opponents don't understand can make you hundreds of thousands of dollars, and I was just going ahead and uploading hour-long videos to explain exactly what I was doing and why to YouTube. A few people noticed and watched, but most people never heard about what I was doing, or didn't realize what it was if they saw it.

If there was ever a "beginning" to me making online content, that was it. I was already constantly online. The Internet connected me to my friends back in New Zealand, and I had developed friend groups on message boards in the early aughts with about as much success as I'd had developing friend groups at school.

It became prohibitively difficult to play online poker in the US in 2011. The US government shut down our ability to play on the sites, my first major collision with nonsensical government policies. The clause which killed online poker in the US was tacked onto a lengthy bill about port security, and when I called my representative, she said that she was concerned that I had been funding terrorists.

At the same time, some family issues had made it difficult for me to travel, and I was getting tired of poker anyway. I'd play games when my savings account started dipping below $60,000 and otherwise find as many other things to do as I could. I spent a couple of years navigating the family problems, a year or so back at university trying to work my way toward a master's in statistics, half a year volunteering at a startup videogame company, and eventually I found myself streaming full-time after the game I'd been working on[7] launched and a couple hundred people tuned into my stream to watch me talk my way through my strategies for playing it. Thus, my career was launched. I dropped out of college for a second time, still degreeless, to dedicate myself to streaming.

_____

7   *Long War 2*, an official mod for *XCOM 2*—the twelfth game in my uncle's favorite *X-COM* franchise.

I jumped from game to game for a while, investing myself heavily in becoming a world-class player of whatever new strategy game caught my eye, then moving on when it grew stale and uncomfortable to keep playing it. My stream really exploded when I found *Slay the Spire*, a single-player card game from a brand-new independent game studio which sold 1.5 million copies and became one of the top 100 video games played on Steam in the year *before* it was even officially released. People found my stream and the videos I made for teaching the game and started calling me the best player in the world. If anyone asked for help learning the game on an online forum, someone would recommend my videos or livestream to them. With that reputation—combined with thousands of hours of work from myself, Hannah, and the other employees, contractors, and volunteers who have supported me—my channel grew quickly, and I became a fairly well-known figure in the world of strategy gaming in general.

Slay the Spire has become even more successful over the last few years, meaning more and more impressive strategy gamers are picking it up and dedicating themselves to it—many after watching my videos! Some of the people who watch my channel see all these other players doing impressive things too, and then ask me if I'm really the best *Slay the Spire* player in the world, which is a fascinating question to be asked. I have never claimed that I am; the title of this chapter is an attempt to sarcastically demonstrate how ludicrous and insufficient it is to summarize someone's life in such a monosyllabic and one-dimensional way. It's like asking Hannah what college she graduated from. All I've ever done with the idea that I'm the best *Spire* player in the world is mock it. If I get incredibly lucky, or make an obvious mistake, I put on a silly voice and say, "He's the best in the world!"

I find it useful to examine this from one of two angles. The first is: Why would anyone care? *Slay the Spire* is a single-player game with no relevant online leaderboards or competitive nature. Whether I'm better than other people at it or not has no effect on the world.

The answer is different for different people, I think, which makes the question all the more perplexing. It's very hard to work out what someone is looking for when they ask. Perhaps they have a different streamer who they're a big fan of and they get excited about the idea that that streamer is the best in the world. Egos can run high in strategy gaming spaces, and believing that your streamer is the "best" might make you feel good when you tell your friends to watch them. I once asked my viewers if they could make a list of people they thought might be the "best" *Spire* players in the world. They managed to name almost everyone who plays *Slay the Spire* with an audience of 500+ people—including a lot of mini-celebrities for whom *Spire* isn't even a main game (presumably most of those suggestions were facetious)—but named zero of the players with audiences of less than 500 people who held or had held world records for the game. I found that hilarious.

Another option is that they might be trying to cite my choices as an argument from authority—or more generally, they might be observing that I make a decision differently from someone else, and wondering which one of us is right. But who the best player in the world is doesn't have all that much to do with who makes a specific decision correctly and who makes it incorrectly. *Slay the Spire* is an extremely complex game, and nobody makes every decision correctly. When people make decisions which are technically incorrect, it is often in the service of a broader strategy which they understand and are able to execute well. Observing one world-class *Slay the Spire* player doing something differently from others is interesting because of the reasons behind their choice, not because it asserts that one way is wrong and the other is correct. More likely, both possible actions are ultimately being done for the wrong—or at least for incompletely explored—reasons, even if one of them is the "correct" button to press. But understanding the reasoning involved in each can help you get closer and closer to thinking about the game, and strategy games more generally—and maybe even life as a whole—correctly.

The second angle is: What does being the best *Slay the Spire* player even mean? *Slay the Spire* isn't played competitively, so there is nothing that everyone is trying to compete at. It has four different characters, and one person might try to do very well on one of them specifically while another tries to do very well on a different one, or as well as they can on all of them. How can you compare one of those players to another, exactly? Some people enjoy trying to chain together the longest streaks of wins that they can manage, and when people cite evidence that I am the "best" they'll often look at the fact that I've played more world record win streaks than anyone else. But other people try their hardest to win each run individually. Someone doing that can have a higher overall win rate than someone who is trying to put together lots of win streaks because the game has no time limit for decision-making. If I spent another four hours per run, I would not generate many win streaks because it would take too long for me to complete each run, but I would have a higher win rate, because every additional hour I spent on close decisions would improve my ability to pick the right option. How do you compare someone who is spending an hour and a half per run to someone who is spending five?

And on top of that, I'm not, at my core, just a *Slay the Spire* player. I am a lot of things, but most of all—and most importantly to someone asking me if I'm really the best *Slay the Spire* player in the world—I am a *Slay the Spire streamer*. The act of watching my stream and otherwise consuming my content isn't simply about *Slay the Spire* expertise; it is about the multitude of things which streaming is.

People use me as a calming voice to fall asleep to and send me requests to make audio recordings of bedtime stories for them, or to center themselves as they recover from panic attacks. People are interested to hear my thoughts on current events, or seek advice from me to help them improve their happiness or productivity. People like my jokes or my trains of thought. People like that I raise money and awareness for causes which are important to them, or which become important to them after they hear my explanations of why they are important to me. When I deflect questions about whether I'm the best *Slay the Spire* player in the world, long-time viewers sometimes say that I am "humble to a fault." They miss that my choice to repeatedly show my audience that I value humility is the point, not a mistake, and is ironically a more impressive trait to highlight than being good at *Slay the Spire* anyway.

Fairly often I'll get a short message from someone thanking me for what I do. They'll say something like, "Hey, I just beat the maximum difficulty of *Slay the Spire*; it would've taken me so much longer without your help! Thank you so much!" I shrug. I'm glad I could be of help. If I think hard about it, I can see that I'm an important guide to a huge ecosystem of more than a million players, but this doesn't actually have all that much to do with the things which are important to me.

But every now and then, I get an email that's several paragraphs long, and the email isn't about *Slay the Spire*. Here's a recent, anonymized example:

"Dear jorbs,

I'm sure this is kind of strange and I second guessed sending you anything at all many times. But I figure the worst that happens is you just never open this email and that's totally fine.

Sometime in the past few years, you had a stream where you started talking about a life coach, or something of the sort, that you were working with. You talked about sitting down with them

44

and you had the task of plotting out what your ideal day looked like. That really sat with me. I started thinking about my ideal day. I remember that because that was about the time I started growing in my life. It feels like your stream and your willingness to share positive and constructive information helped me start.

Back then, I was working six days a week at a small restaurant as a waiter. It was fine but it definitely was not my ideal. Now I am working full time in software development and much more efficient with my time. And I can't help but trace back that I started changing direction toward this work I am much more passionate about back to you sharing a piece of yourself.

This isn't my only example of you having positive change on my life, but I do feel like it is the most profound. I appreciate you being a positive change for me, whether you meant to be or not.

So thank you! Sometimes I see your streams and feel like a lot weighs on you so I decided to send this, in hopes that it will give you back some of the positivity you have given me."

Now, that email makes me tear up.[8] That email is about the thing that I achieve in the world. And so when someone asks me if I'm the best *Slay the Spire* player, the main thing I think is that they're asking the wrong question. This isn't uncommon—it's very typical in this world to ask the wrong question. We live in structured rulesets which tell us what is important and how we should behave, and the questions we ask are both the products of these structures and the reinforcements of their hold over us. But the paradigmatic shifts in our lives and in our societies happen not when people start giving different answers, but when they start asking different questions, and every day I try to give people reasons to re-examine the questions they are asking. It might be

---

8   I picked one that was easy to read for the sake of the book, but I'd like to add that the ones from people who are clearly getting help from Google Translate to compose a written message in English usually make me start ugly-crying.

as simple as changing "What restaurant should I eat at tonight?" into "What ritual of getting and eating food would make me happiest?" Take that second question and attack it with some friends and some deliberate habit-forming, and you might be amazed by what happens.

And stop asking who the best player of a single-player strategy game is when you're trying to decide which stream to watch. Ask which stream will bring you the most joy, or comfort, or challenge, or thought, or learning. Or, honestly, maybe it'd be a good time to go outside for a bit.

Back in university, I took some computer science courses and tried being a programmer like my dad. I taught classes and summer camps like my grandmother. But as an adult, I worked out that my real calling, the thing I wanted most, was to be a boat. Which obviously doesn't make sense; people can't be boats. But we don't quite have the right words for what it is when a person is a boat yet, so it's the best I've got. I want to be a vessel for the excellence of others. I want to carry them to a place where they belong, and provide shelter in harbor for them when they need to rest. I want to endure storms, and heat, and cold, while they are comfortable and safe below deck. The community I have built online is a boat ferrying passengers to their destinations across our generation's online frontier, and I am not so much its captain as I am its hull.

A LIMINAL WORLD

I sat down to write a liminal work, mostly because I thought that was what smart guys with important things to say did, and I found the word funny. A liminal memoir from the Pacific Northwest seemed like almost as iconic a cliché as a disruptive technology from San Francisco. I'd jokingly tell my friends that what I was writing was liminal, and they would sigh and roll their eyes. This was once a fairly light-hearted endeavor.

Literally, "liminal" means changing, or crossing a threshold. It's from the Latin word for "threshold," which is how I was originally introduced to the word, back in classics courses in university. It sounds very exciting and happening, evoking imagery of newlyweds walking into the next phase of their lives together, or superheroes in movies and TV shows ascending out of adversity and putting on a slightly differently colored outfit. The world of streaming seems liminal enough. I imagine the word came up a lot in investment meetings when John was trying to convince people who didn't know any better to give him hundreds of thousands of dollars, for example.

But the more I wrote, the more I realized that the word is terrifying. In a liminal space like this, anything could change at any time. One morning I woke up and Twitch's largest competitor, Microsoft's streaming platform Mixer, had been shut down overnight. There wasn't an announcement that they were scaling down or anything; they just completely took the website offline. As of this book's publication, the URL redirects to Facebook Gaming, but who knows if that will still exist a year from now. Hardly a reassuring thought for a person who has spent seven years of his life building a career centered on these websites.

In a space like this, the people I trust most are the ones who are strong, unfaltering, and worthy. Hannah is one of those people. Her motivations don't change moment-to-moment—she wakes up every morning and wants to be kind to people and take care of those around her. Another one of those people is a tall, handsome, and unrepentantly crass redheaded man who goes by the online moniker "FilthyRobot" and likes to make gratuitous sex jokes and destroy people at strategy games. He was the first established streamer who respected and cared about me, which meant a lot to me then and still does now.

At this point I've been streaming for seven years, and I've tried to pay the favor forward many times. I reach out to people who are starting out and tell them I enjoy their content, and then I sit and chat with them for an hour or two about streaming and the things to watch out for and the things that I enjoy doing to make myself happiest. Boundary-setting, community-building, things like that. There are no clear rules or goals in the streaming world, and it's important to me to make sure someone who is trying to build their own stream realizes that and picks rules and goals which work for them.

When Filthy reached out to me, I was still quite new to streaming. He'd seen my content for *Long War 2* and was interested in playing the game himself. He was impressed that I was succeeding at the game with an approach he hadn't seen from other streamers. He wanted to help give me a platform to continue what I was doing, and hopefully learn from me himself. So, he asked me if I'd be interested in joining him on his channel to explain some of the mechanics to him and his audience. We ground through a few hours of the game. I had worked on it, loved it, and knew more about it than almost anyone in the world, but even I can admit that it was a painful and tedious game to play and to learn. Loading screens could easily take two minutes to complete; I literally told our viewers (and Filthy!) stories from *Arabian Nights* to pass the time.

After we gave up on our *Long War 2* playthrough, we continued to chat offline and eventually started playing *Dungeons & Dragons* and other games together. I met him and his wife when they visited the Pacific Northwest, and we all went hiking together. When I joined F2K, I chatted with Filthy about it, and he ended up joining as well in the same month. We spent long afternoon and evening calls relaxing and shooting the shit about the team, streaming, and life in general.

We are an odd couple. He is brutally honest, and I always expect him to say exactly what he feels. We both took the same personality test once—the male strategy gamer's version of doing horoscopes together, I guess—and it gave us almost identical personality traits except that I was in the ninetieth percentile for agreeableness and he was in the tenth.

The pinnacle of Filthy's brand, in my opinion, was when Wizards of the Coast passed him over for an invite to a *Magic: The Gathering* invitational despite his having streamed their game heavily for several months and being one of the most watched channels for it on Twitch. He saw many other streamers—including some with significantly smaller channels than his—getting invited to the tournament, which paid $7,500 even if you didn't win any matches, and $250,000 for first place. He was pissed. When he asked why he was being excluded from this potentially life-changing event for a game he had dedicated the last six months of his life and his channel to, he received a canned PR response to the effect that "there had been many motivations for who was picked." On the day of the tournament, he had a friend jump onto his channel with him, they opened some beers, and he spent the entire day shit-talking about Wizards of the Coast.[9]

Here's where it gets truly beautiful: Wizards ended their tournament with ten thousand or so viewers. When a stream ends, it's normal to host another channel, which will send all of the viewers watching your channel to that other stream. It's a cool way to recommend other streamers you watch to your audience and immediately send them to check those streamers out. I don't know exactly why Filthy didn't get invited to the tournament, but he clearly didn't have enough of a black flag on his channel to be a complete outcast with Wizards yet. Pretty much everyone else in the *Magic: The Gathering* streaming ecosystem had been playing the tournament, so his channel was by far the second-most-watched channel for the game. Whoever was in charge of the broadcast decided to host him.

So, he's sitting there, having a few drinks, and he receives the largest host that his channel has ever received. It's from Wizards of the Coast. Usual etiquette here is to say, "Hey whoa, thanks for the host!" or something like that. He just kept on shit-talking about Wizards of the Coast nonstop for several more hours instead, to ten thousand or so people who had just come from their official broadcast.

I appreciate and love that Filthy does things like this. They take a while to understand, but once you do understand them, you can understand him as an incredibly honest and straight-forward human being. It's his flavor of integrity. And really, the world could use a lot more people who use the largest windfall they've ever had in their careers to tell the corporation that brought it to them to go fuck itself.

---

9   It is plausible to me that his belief that he should do things like this in response to perceived injustice is why a large corporation didn't want to invite him to their event.

I am significantly less honest than Filthy is. I go out of my way to try to frame things in kindness and love, which is arguably noble but can also lead to dishonesty. In this book I do say honest things about how I feel about other people. Sometimes I even say things I'd consider cruel about them. But I honestly think some of the people you're going to read about are destroying the planet and all of humanity and should be run out of society, and I certainly don't go so far as to say that very often.

One time, we were playing a *D&D* session and had a new player in the group for the day. At the end of the session, Filthy asked me how I'd enjoyed playing with them, wondering if he should invite them back, and I said that it was fun and that I'd be happy to play with them again. Then he asked me if that was really what I thought, and I said, "Yes!" He asked me to say one mean thing about them, and I said that I didn't really want to do that. He kept pushing me for five minutes or so as I continued deflecting. Eventually he broke me, and I admitted that I hadn't enjoyed playing with them much at all and had thought none of their jokes were funny and that I would rather never play with them again.

Curiously, Filthy and I seem to largely make the same life decisions. We arguably connected over being good at strategy games more than our personalities, and our decisions are motivated by those sub-personality traits and end up often matching. I've been raised to believe that personality matters, that communication should be both honest and kind, and that I should treat others with respect, but in my own life I've noticed that the personalities and mannerisms of the people I know don't necessarily matter all that much. Some people who are incredibly kind to me have betrayed me or failed me, while some of the people who treat me with cruelty have come through consistently with incredible opportunities or advice.

I think of Filthy as an "anti-liminal" goliath. He bluntly and resolutely remains true to himself, no matter the circumstance. If the world changes, he will watch it go by. These goliaths—I know a few—aren't perfect. What they are is reliably *themselves*, and it's possible for people to look at them and agree about what that means.

The counterpart to the anti-liminal goliath is the two-faced grifter, eager to capitalize on change: the person who doesn't care about you unless you're useful to them, who developed their moral compass at business school or somewhere comparable and finds it reliably points toward money and power over all else. Commonly, they are people who know enough about economics to know that it often assumes humans will act rationally to maximize their wealth, but not enough about economics to know that the assumption isn't true in the real world and is just used to aid pursuit of knowledge in the field. And certainly they don't know enough about ethics to recognize that they have to analyze their own actions and work out how to not act as greedy assholes.

And so, after that regretfully biased introduction, we should take an interlude to meet Cody, F2K's president, chairman, and angel investor. The two main startup terms that I learned in my time at F2K were "unicorn"—"a thing which cannot possibly happen, but which would make us lots of money if it did"—and "angel investor"—"a person who pays for us to dress up as a unicorn."

I am being slightly unfair. F2K had, at all times, a vision of something which could possibly happen which would make it lots of money. That's an important narrative to sell yourself for investment rounds. F2K just never actually made convincing, concrete steps toward making these things come true. There was always talk about them, and claims we'd make progress on them when we had spare funds and time, but then if we ever had spare funds and time, we failed to follow through convincingly on them. At times we ran small tournament series, or built community networks of streamers, but they never succeeded in the ways we were hoping they would.

When I left, the big thing was pack opening—F2K said that it would build a warehouse in the States which would be a central hub for content creators to get packs for pack-opening content from, and then they could send the packs back to the warehouse for the cards to be graded and sent out to viewers who purchased them from the streamer. Pack opening is a tiny blip in the world of online content creation, but occasionally it's quite profitable, and Cody's girlfriend—a small streamer—had started testing it out on her stream with some success, so all of a sudden, it was what the entire company was about.

Pack opening is one of my least favorite types of content in the online space. The Internet has been around long enough now that there are people who have lived surrounded by its predatory behaviors their entire lives, such that they forgivably assume that those behaviors are valid and permissible. Packs of cards for use in trading card games are just slot machines marketed at children, and their videogame equivalents are often even worse. They're ethically and intellectually bankrupt, and exist entirely because of the way they manipulate a player's (or viewer's, or streamer's!) dopamine.

Manipulative design is all over the Internet. When you refresh Twitter and notice that the number of notifications you have doesn't show up straight away, the delay creates a dopamine response which mirrors a slot machine (why do slot machines have a short delay before you find out whether you won or not?) and addicts you to the website. The actual act of clicking on the notification button to see what your notifications are is a little dopamine button, too. Seeing "new tweets" on your timeline and being able to click to see what they are is a dopamine button.

These tricks are part of how the site keeps your attention so it can sell you advertising and gather data about you.

One of the problems with a person or organization not having a consistent vision, moral compass, personality—take your pick, really—is that these things become malleable enough to connect with whatever next big thing you might want to pursue. An organization which claims to be about the promotion of women in the online gaming space can ignore its only female staff member and employ a bunch of sexist men, because nobody is actually checking whether it is doing the thing it says it's doing or not. And then the second the empowerment of women stops being a hot selling point to investors, the masks swap and the organization can now be about capitalizing on a type of content which is taking off because it's addictive to children. That your first goal was ethical and commendable was surface-level and coincidental. Throughout my time with F2K, the organization was a mix of visionary with no follow-through and reactionary with no relevance, treating ethical direction as a luxury reserved for whenever it was chic or we had cash on hand.

But the team couldn't exist without money, and even with all of its ethical flexibility, its business model didn't make much money without outside help. The structure of money in the online space is something like:

1. Big rich person or company has lots of money and thinks the online space is going to blow up, so they invest the money.

2. Some startup gets the money. They don't have a sustainable business model, but they have an idea for how to accrue lots of attention. When people from San Francisco talk about it, they use the word "disruptive." Think about Netflix in its early days, sending DVDs to people for free. Great idea, lots of value to people, *absolutely* not profitable or sustainable.

But Netflix managed to turn it into something else; good for them.

3. The startup flips the switch. Suddenly they aren't about growth anymore; they're about profit. If everything goes right, now they're making money.

This is a simultaneously fascinating and ridiculous space to navigate as an individual running your own small business. There are some very clear exploitative strategies one could use. For example, you could take advantage of the startups which are burning through a million dollars to try to get attention, use the services they provide without actually ever creating any reliance on them, then cancel your account when they start trying to charge more.

This is a common strategy all over this space. At one point, when F2K partnered with a for-profit charity middleman, there was a lot of conversation about whether we were going to be out of the deal before they flipped the switches to start making millions of dollars off of people's charity work. Never mind, of course, that supporting them on their way to that point was horribly unethical already.

The intruding startup's counterstrategy is to try to get so much of the market share that customers have no choice but to stay with them when they flip into money mode, but almost every company I've seen in the space has completely failed at this. Twitch and YouTube arguably did an okay job of it, although there's a bit of complexity behind the scenes there.

The basic problem with step three—converting your platform into a cash cow—is that there are too many people eager to invest in the space. If you try to have a sustainable business model, someone else will just mosey on over and undercut you with one that isn't sustainable, and all of a sudden you'll be yesterday's news. Yesterday's news doesn't have much success on the Internet.

So, how does F2K, a company which at some point had a sort of profitable model, but which has struggled to maintain relevance or land anything big, continue to exist in this space? Well, one way is for someone to pay lots of money so that it can.

**

John and Cody go way back. While John was ascending through the ranks of *Hearthstone*, Cody settled into poker online, winning himself a small fortune. Cody had been relaxing by watching John stream his *Hearthstone* games, and when John wanted to start his own team, they connected.

Online poker may be a space even more rife with confusion and misunderstanding than streaming. For starters, poker isn't gambling like a slot machine is. It's a strategy game where people place bets using chips and it's possible to connect money to those chips, either directly or indirectly. There are poker tournaments where people pay an entry fee and then receive a payout based on how far they get before they lose all their chips. These tournaments have the same structure as the *Magic: The Gathering* tournaments which our society was okay with me entering when I was a kid.

One question that follows: Is the sensible conclusion that poker *isn't* gambling, or is it just that other strategy games played for prizes are gambling, too? I'd tend more toward the latter conclusion than the former, but it comes down to how you define gambling. Does a player's skill decide whether they win or lose? In poker, worse players may get lucky for a while—even long enough to win an entire tournament—but better players will always defeat them in the long run. When I express that poker isn't gambling, I mean that it's no more like gambling than a lot of other things which are central to our lives—Twitter, dating apps, maybe even getting or avoiding zits. Gambling sells well, and modeling your website or game after a casino is a successful way to retain attention.

Does that mean any of this is okay, from an ethical standpoint? No, almost certainly not. I struggled to justify my career while I was a poker player, and have no desire to return to anything like it

That isn't even the juicy half of misunderstanding online poker. Most people think that poker is about reading your opponent or the luck of the draw. The reality is that it's a relatively simple strategy game about placing the right bets at the right times in order to make money. Betting with a balanced range of both strong hands and bluffs mathematically increases the percentage of the pot that you are expected to win. Your opponent has no counterplay because most of their hands aren't worth calling against your hands that beat them—meaning that they have no way of consistently stopping your bluffs. If they choose to call all the time, they pay off your good hands, which is too high a price to pay for stopping your bluffs. Either way, you make money. Nowadays we have computer programs which can solve exactly how you should do this in most hands of No-Limit Hold'em.

I myself came up through online poker in 2008-2011, which was the tail end of its golden age. Money was *everywhere*, and almost nobody had a clue what they were doing. I'd been playing strategy games my entire life and did quite well, enough so that I could coast through the rest of my twenties off my savings (with some help from my parents—thanks, Mum and Dad!) and eventually build a successful streaming career.

One thing that's tricky about poker is that when most people talk about poker strategy, they are talking exclusively about how to win at the table you're sitting at. They start with these questions: What are your opponents like? How much money does everyone have in play? And so on. Relatively few people— even successful professionals—recognize and react sensibly to how important it is to sit at the right table to begin with.

Everybody understands that sitting near someone who's making a lot of mistakes is profitable, but very few poker players spend even 5% of their energy on trying to find such players who want to play with them.

Perhaps one reason is that selecting opponents is distasteful. People want to believe that poker is a pristine strategy game, and certainly the strategy involved in it is intricate and perfect and blameless. People with math PhDs can get lost in it for years. But it's also a messy world about knowing the right people in order to get a seat at the right table. Players with social elegance can even find ways to make the distastefulness of this go away. While a strategy purist crassly refers to weaker players as "fish" or "whales" to be preyed upon—constructing a world in which they are superior to the players they beat and therefore deserve their money—a more socially adept player may beautifully evoke the enjoyment of competition and the satisfaction of being tested against some of the world's best poker players, even at a loss. While a concerned onlooker makes noise about gambling addiction and families torn apart by parents losing everything they have, a more socially adept player strikes up a friendship with Guy Laliberté (founder of Cirque du Soleil, net worth 1.2 billion) and shows him how fun it is to play poker with some big personalities who compete at it for a living every now and then.

It was hard to even criticize Laliberté's play as being full of "mistakes" when he did things like giving opponents back $70,000 because he didn't want them to feel bad and didn't want to put them under financial pressure. That is obviously mathematically incorrect for profit maximization, but it surpasses the point where the term "mistake" makes any sense. He eventually stopped playing poker, I'm pretty sure because a bunch of the strategy purists who weren't invited to the games he was in were making fun of him.

One can choose to believe that any of these visions of poker are true, and how a poker player justifies (or grimaces at) their own profession is as much a matter of how they choose to think and act on that day as anything else.

The way a company like F2K might go about courting investors seemed like it could have many similarities to the world of poker, so I was anticipating an interesting conversation as I made the Skype pilgrimage to meet Cody, the successful poker player who owned most of the company. I've never quite understood why John liked introducing me to other people. Perhaps he liked me and thought I was an impressive person to introduce to others. Maybe, for a while, he was trying to convince me to join him in scamming other people. Maybe he'd worked out that I liked meeting cool people and was using it as a slow drip to control me. Maybe I was just a show horse. Whatever it was, for my part, I was interested to learn a bit more about the back end of the company, so when John offered me the chance to meet Cody, I jumped at it.

Far from moving on from poker in 2011 like I had, Cody had doubled down and was still competing in the largest games.[10] In our conversation, I didn't exactly get a good vibe. He did not seem like he was trying very hard to justify his profession of taking money off other people. In fact, he was trying to code bots in order to automate the process, and I'd heard some ideas from John about using data from F2K to create and sell algorithms to

_____

10 I wonder somewhat often what my life would have been like if I'd lived outside the United States in 2011. My family, my partner, and my partner's families were all in the States, so it was hard for me to travel to continue playing, and that made it much easier to quit entirely than I might have found it otherwise. It's possible that the day I woke up and found out that the poker site holding ~80% of my net worth had been taken down by the US government was the luckiest day of my life.

predict stream metrics which implied that Cody was trying to bring that mindset into our team.

I began the conversation by mentioning my interest in doing charity work, and we derailed completely and immediately. Cody expressed that his idea of doing good in the world was to make lots of money so that thirty years from now, he could have tens of millions of dollars to fund whatever cause the world needed, which is still one of the most bizarre ideas of ethical behavior that I've ever heard. What if the world needs you to not hoard money and instead be good and kind to others *now*, Cody?

I was still almost okay with Cody's position at the time. I didn't agree with the idea, but at least it was a premise couched in a desire to do good in the world. We really derailed when Cody started arguing that streamers should be doing the same thing—that the streamers who would be able to do the most good in the world were the ones who could do a good job of selling themselves and acting as chameleons who'd fit into promotions for all sorts of different products, so that they could make as much money as possible.

I do not think that's what makes a streamer successful at generating money, let alone what allows a streamer to achieve good in the world. In his view, basing the entire industry on deceit was a good thing because the people profiting from it would use the money well later.

My understanding of the success of streamers, in contrast, is based on authenticity. I am transparent with my audience. I tell them what I really think, and I try to only bring advertising to the channel that I think they are well-served in seeing. This has been the mechanic through which I have succeeded as a streamer. There is a disparity in how I, as a streamer, am judged by the world, compared to how Cody is judged as an investor. Streaming makes me very visible; at any moment, someone can look up the best and worst moments of the last five years of my life, and use them to decide whether I am a good or bad person. But they can't do that for Cody. Cody might never be judged—or if he is, perhaps it will be in a carefully crafted eulogy which highlights his successes and sees no reason to acknowledge any of his failures or cruelties.

After that conversation, I was never invited to speak with Cody again. Most of the time, he was reclusive and focused on his own projects, other than occasionally dishing out another hundred thousand dollars for operational costs. I'm sure the way that he interacted with F2K was muddied by the fact that he held the majority of shares in it and wanted it to succeed despite being largely removed a lot of the time. On occasion, he came in to work in the upper tiers of the company for a while, but at other times he disappeared and stopped responding to messages. Whatever Cody's actual involvement at a given time, John was quick to leverage their friendship toward F2K's success (and, by extension, John's own success as CEO). I don't remember seeing any evidence that John had anything in his life that he wasn't prepared to leverage for his own gain.

But, while I haven't spoken with Cody again, I have definitely spoken with people *like* Cody since then: investors who are removed from the space, don't really understand what's going on, and expect me to help them maximize their profits. Who think that I'll sign up to sell my viewers slot machines for children because that's what's making money right now. Whose ethical foundations are impossible to examine—because they don't seem to have any.

One of the bizarre asymmetries in streaming is that a team like F2K is beholden to shareholders who demand profit margins, but the streamers themselves are contractors for whom the team provides only a small segment of their overall revenue. Maybe 20% of what I made at that time came through F2K, and I made significantly more than I needed. Without any personal mandate to maximize my earnings, I had no reason to bend over backward or sell myself in ways I was uncomfortable with just to make F2K happy. And so, in a space where people yearn for genuine positivity and connection, F2K's "team" atmosphere was more like a revolving door: new, incoming talent who were excited to sign with an org—who thought this was "making it"—and disgruntled talent leaving after a year or two because their uniqueness was not valued, their vision no longer matched the company's, and they had been mistreated and herded into sponsorship agreements that they didn't need or like.

PUTTING OUT FIRES

Sometimes people tell me that they don't understand how streaming can be hard. If I ever express that I'm stressed out or tired or feeling negative in any other way, there will be one or two people eager to tell me that I should be thankful that all I have to do for a living is play video games. I'm sometimes asked what my "real job" is at the tail-end of an eight-hour-long stream to three thousand live viewers.

Throughout this book, I speak at length about the ins and outs of the backend of my job, but I don't spend too long talking about the stress involved in the frontend. Ironically, while I'm writing mainly about the backend, for the last three years the administrative background tasks involved in my stream have been managed almost entirely by Hannah, and so this book is mostly about parts of my job that I'm now somewhat isolated from. The backend stuff still affects me, sure, but—like when Hannah found herself caricaturing Dale and his Igor—it now feels sort of like watching a reality TV show. When Hannah and I were first getting to know each other, we had a funny cultural exchange moment when I told her that I got quite a lot of schadenfreude out of watching things unfold on the backend of streaming, and she told me she got a lot of kuyashii from it, and neither of us knew what the other meant.[11]

---

11 Schadenfreude is a German word meaning pleasure derived from seeing someone else fail in a way that you feel they deserve. Kuyashii is a Japanese word meaning a burning desire to prove that someone who doubts you is wrong. I had a moment of embarrassed regret acknowledging that I felt something so crass in response to the same situations

It's much more difficult for me to talk about the stress involved in actually streaming live to thousands of people, forty or more hours a week, day in, day out. It feels immediately real and personal.

Streaming is very much a job about building momentum. I often compare the online entertainment world to surfing: lots of calm holding-pattern actions while waiting for the next big thing, and then a new game gets released or a new scandal hits or a new trend emerges and everyone tries to hop on their surfboards and catch the wave. The larger your channel and the more experienced you are, the easier this becomes.

The grind is very real, though. Some stats on my streaming career are publicly available,[12] and they show the amount of work I've put into this. In the last 1,639 days (at the time of writing this draft), I have streamed 9,712 hours, which adds up to a little under six hours per day or a little over forty hours per week. That's how many hours my stream has been live. It doesn't count: setting up my studio; email, Discord, and Twitter conversations; recording content exclusively for YouTube; fulfilling my backend responsibilities; building and managing a Discord server with several thousand members; managing business relationships with employees and contractors; or attending conventions. (Or writing a book.) You get the idea. The rates above aren't excluding weeks taken off for vacation—mostly I haven't had those. My stream has been live at some point on 91.3% of the calendar days in this time period—a slightly exaggerated statistic because it

---

that filled Hannah's life with a noble fire, but she reassured me it was good that I had a functional coping mechanism. My enjoyment of schadenfreude has diminished as I've worked on this book. The feeling is a luxury only experienced by someone who is detached or protected from the pain of the failures they're observing, and at some point it stopped working well for me.

12 See www.twitchtracker.com/jorbs/statistics.

counts streams which went past midnight as being live for the next calendar day, as well. It's still a ridiculous number—and it's probably unhealthy that I regularly stream past midnight.

There is a Twitter account which posts a GIF of Daniel Craig introducing the Weeknd on *Saturday Night Live* every Friday afternoon with "Ladies and gentlemen, the weekend!" subtitled on it. I often joke that I am slowly building a Pavlovian response to that GIF which delivers all of the recuperation and rest of taking two days off so that I never have to actually stop working. Even if I do take a day off, I'm often talking to my friends about my job, or playing games offline and thinking about how I could create content about them. There's rarely a real break from streaming, at least not in my experience.

Sometime in the nineties and early aughts, some corporations worked out how to make money off of people attaching a webcam and microphone to their computer and streaming themselves playing games in their bedrooms. While this has afforded me wonderful experiences in my own life, I still can't help but feel like it's an incredibly invasive and grotesque opportunity to present to a teenager. It's hard not to feel somewhat betrayed and failed by a society which let that happen to me and is still letting that happen to my friends' children as they grow up in a world saturated by the Internet.

The biggest lie in streaming is that you will succeed. Twitch presents new streamers with a pathway to becoming a Twitch affiliate, and they make this step quite attainable. Stream seven times in thirty days for a total of five hundred minutes. Average at least three viewers over that time period. Have at least fifty followers. Do these things, and you can start "making money"— but it's barely anything, and you won't actually receive a payout until you've accumulated $50[13] in earnings. In the meanwhile,

---

13   Reduced from $100, which it was before 2022.

Twitch, which is a subsidiary of Amazon, will happily profit from the advertising revenue generated by your channel.[14]

Once you're a Twitch affiliate, you're presented with the much more difficult pathway to becoming a partner. Twelve streams totaling twenty-five hours in the last thirty days, averaging at least seventy-five viewers, will make you eligible to apply, although Twitch may reject your application.[15] And even if you are accepted, all you really get is a more exclusive contract and a check mark next to your name. Most Twitch partners still make significantly less than minimum wage, and the vast majority of people who try to stream on Twitch never make it to partnership at all. In 2019, a LEGO survey of kids between the ages of eight to twelve found that about 30% of them wanted to be content creators,[16] and the second they turned thirteen those kids were allowed to make Twitch accounts and start down that path. In

---

14 Twitch recently started letting viewers subscribe to channels for multiple months at once. So instead of paying $5 for a monthly subscription, they can pay $60 for a yearly subscription, for example. The problem is that our contracts say we're meant to be paid our share of revenue by some period of time after it comes in, but Twitch will hold the $60 for an entire year, giving us our share of the $5 monthly fee every month, even though they've been holding the $60 they received for twelve months by the time we get the last fraction of it that we're entitled to. I'm fairly sure this is not what it says in my contract, but, uh . . . who am I going to take that to, exactly? One does not get the sense that anyone cares very much.

15 To my knowledge, there is no oversight as to whether Twitch's process for reviewing partner applications respects the sort of labor laws meant to be followed by companies considering employee applications. It would honestly shock me if, for example, a traditionally attractive woman who streamed with her webcam on wasn't more likely to be accepted for partnership than a woman who streamed without a webcam. Again, it's unclear there is any organization, governmental or otherwise, which is doing anything about this.

16 About three times the 11% who wanted to be astronauts.

a more reasonable world, we might identify this as exploitative child labor.

In spite of the grind, I do have a few sacred hours in my week. I spend time in groups of streamers who understand that nothing we do together is about our streams; instead, we goof off in a video call or play *D&D*. I used to take walks with my partner—until our dual anxieties exploded a couple of years into me entertaining a hundred thousand people through a global pandemic, and we broke up; now I go on walks by myself. I'm not going to talk much about those hours here because, like I said, they are sacred, and they are for me, not for anyone else. If I didn't have moments which were just for me, I would probably implode into nothingness under the pressure of everything else around me, as I monetize and commodify the experiences of my life to create hundreds of hours of entertainment every month.

In a recent conversation with FilthyRobot, he lamented that when he started streaming at age 29, he had half a lifetime of experiences to draw entertaining stories, facts, and beliefs from. Now, at 37, he has almost fully turned that interesting lifetime into content already, and has added comparatively few interesting experiences to draw from in the last eight years,[17] which have been mostly spent at a computer in a room with soft green walls and dark curtains over the windows, talking into a microphone.

***

---

17 Or at least, relatively few that either of us would feel comfortable talking about in a live show. You will notice that I have plenty to talk about in a book, but that is because I spend most of my life feeling an unresolvable friction between the urge to turn everything interesting about myself into content and the recognition that some things are too sensitive to talk about in front of a live audience. Eventually, one day, I sat down and started writing things I wished I could find the right way to say, but had been avoiding, and the full first draft of this book flowed out of my fingers in about two weeks.

Beyond the general miasma of streaming, the day-to-day stressors start to blur together so much that I found I couldn't even organize them in my head to make a list of them for you. I reached out to friends to ask for help coming up with examples. It's okay to just decide you believe me and skip to the next chapter if you'd like. None of this list is fun to read, but it may be useful for getting a sense of what our society's thirteen-year-olds are dealing with at work.

Many bad experiences have to do with viewers misunderstanding and crossing boundaries, sometimes in extremely particular ways. One streamer shared that a viewer said they were in love with them on the second or third stream they ever did, which led to a panicked response—they didn't want that sort of connection in streaming in any way. They found a good way to deal with it eventually: making bot commands which explained that that sort of comment was inappropriate in their community.

I call this "canonizing" something about your community. Live shows are in constant flux: sometimes it's time for jokes; sometimes it's time to focus; sometimes it's time to speak seriously about a topic. But we all have our own boundaries which are constant, and setting and enforcing them is hard to do within the infrastructure of Twitch, which only provides a single "chat rules" pop-up that most viewers don't even read before arriving in our chat, free to send messages. As an example, I've canonized explanations about how I don't like "backseating" (from the phrase "backseat driving"), which is what we call it when people suggest what decision you should make in a game you're playing.

Ironically, I first started streaming because of how much I enjoyed interacting with backseaters. I had been uploading some *XCOM* videos to YouTube, and after an upload I always enjoyed checking the comments the next day and getting into conversations with viewers about why I'd made certain decisions.

I figured if I streamed live, I'd be able to have those conversations in real time.

These conversations were fun when I was having them with a few people I recognized, but, as my channel grew, they started to become shallow and taxing, and eventually I found myself starting to have stress responses to difficult decisions. I knew that instead of getting to think through them, I was going to be bombarded by fifty different people giving me three-word opinions on what they thought I should do. My breathing would get shallow, and I would feel like my chest was floating. My eyes would lose focus a little, and I would look over at my chat window, already knowing that I was going to hate what I would see. Parts of my body would clench up—my jaw, my feet, my shoulders—and sometimes I wouldn't have the presence of mind to relax them until they started painfully cramping an hour later. When I tried to explain what was going on, people would make ludicrous suggestions like "Just don't read the chat," as though I could reasonably stop interacting with the community I had built and whom I entertained for my job.

I had to fix this if I wanted to continue doing this job. So I made automated chatbot responses telling people not to backseat, and set filters to keep messages containing certain words from appearing in my chat feed. I recorded a thirty-minute video explaining my feelings on backseating and spent two months working through the stress response I was having with a therapist. I explained what was going on to my moderators, setting my chat window to a four-second delay so they would have time to delete messages before I ever saw them. When I decided to stop allowing backseating, I was told daily, for the next six months, that it was a bad decision and that I didn't understand that it was a vital part of the streaming experience.[18] That's how much pain, time, and

18   My viewership, overall, went up.

effort it took me to canonize one thing about my community. There are still constant miscommunications in which someone backseats without realizing it and then gets upset when their message is deleted.

A big issue with having a hundred thousand people following your channel is that the person acting worst is always the one who stands out. Probably 95% of my viewers had no issue with me making a rule against backseating, and the vast majority of those who didn't like the new rule silently moved on to watch someone else, or else made their peace with my decision and continued to watch my channel, obeying the new rules. But the viewer I'll always remember is the guy who blew up at me and my moderators, called us Nazis, got banned from my Twitch channel, went to Twitter and started replying to my tweets with accusations that I was a fascist, emailed me about how upset he was, then got into the community's Discord, wrote a long diatribe about how unfair I was being, and then direct messaged me my previous home address.

Doing things differently from usual can end up getting a lot of unwanted attention on the Internet. One friend shared an experience where he was given new *Magic: The Gathering* cards to preview, and his team decided to preview them at the end of the show instead of the start, and a subsection of the *Magic: The Gathering* community started a harassment campaign against them. Dealing with individuals acting out is awful; being targeted by an entire mob is even worse. Twitter has this awful functionality that allows you to retweet your own reply to a tweet, which takes it out of its original context and puts it in front of everyone who follows you. So a person can suddenly be on the receiving end of two hundred thousand Twitter users—who didn't read the original context of their tweet— responding to another user telling them they should get mad at or make fun of them.

These mobs don't always target the streamers themselves—a *Hearthstone* streamer shared about the time a hundred or so people found his fifteen-year-old sister's Facebook account and decided to gang up on her.

My experience as a content creator has felt like arriving as a unique and interesting piece of wood, and then being put on a lathe and perfectly smoothed into an inoffensive wooden sphere. I've learned automatic answers to questions which I give because I know they're acceptable rather than because I've ever bothered to consider whether I agree with them or not. I'm not an epidemiologist or science communicator, but I sure had to learn what the "right" response was to people asking me questions about the coronavirus—and by "right" I mean the one which wouldn't result in anyone threatening to hurt my family.[19] Many of the peculiar opinions I have—the ones which make me feel like I have something unique to offer my viewers to begin with—feel exhausting to explain for the thousandth time in a seven-year career, especially when I know I'm going to have to deal with the one person in several thousand who responds to them the most negative way possible, and so I've stopped looking forward to mentioning them.

Some of the experiences that smaller streamers have had are particularly nasty, and I think I was mostly fortunate to dodge them while I was establishing myself on Twitch. There's a personal boundary which starts to exist when a streamer's audience gets large enough, which (I believe) makes a twisted and miserable human being stop believing that they can affect

---

19 I perhaps do myself slight disservice here. I also reached out to researchers at the beginning of the pandemic, spent maybe forty hours educating myself about what was going on, and even had scientists from the University of Washington join me on the channel to talk about the virus and show viewers a computer game which would explore ways to fold proteins that might be able to neutralize the virus.

them. And so, as someone with 100,000 followers, I am mostly left alone by people trying to make personal attacks—I no longer seem accessible or vulnerable. In comparison, a friend of mine shared a story about his stream where he celebrated reaching a thousand followers. The thousandth follower was someone who said that they knew him and asked him to check his Instagram DMs, where he found pictures of people self-harming and suicide. After the obvious ban, that person made five more accounts to try as hard as they could to ruin the celebration stream. Another friend shared that, at a similar channel size, someone came into his chat after losing a game against him and spent an hour attacking him, constantly making new accounts with different names. He found "IPissOnYourGrandfathersGrave" to be particularly upsetting, as he was struggling with the anniversary of his grandfather's death.

I did have a couple of longer-term experiences with extremely manipulative viewers, mostly while I was getting established. One donated quite a lot of money to the channel, but while doing so, tried to press further and further past my boundaries, asking to do things like rent an apartment for me and posting more and more inappropriate sexual messages in chat. I eventually banned him when he DMed me something sexual on one of my days off.

Another shared stories about his struggles with substance abuse and suicidal thoughts and manipulated myself and many of the other central members of my community into doing him favors. These included requests for money, requests for people to talk to, and requests to be made a moderator so that he could have some sort of responsibility in his life. I decided to try letting him moderate, and he started directing gun emotes at people who were participating in chat in ways he didn't like (but which weren't even against the rules).

After I removed his moderator status, he sent me messages about how upset he was that he'd failed even at that, and then continued requesting to be given a second chance as a moderator for months afterward and told sob stories to other central members of my community, soliciting money from them and trying to get them to recommend that I reinstate him—as though my moderation team existed to serve his personal quest instead of being my trusted tool for keeping toxicity *out* of my channel. He still pops up in the channel every now and then, and I always find myself immediately on edge, wondering if he's going to try to redirect conversation away from the game I'm playing in front of two thousand people and onto his struggle with substance abuse. Viewers who toe the line, never quite doing anything wrong enough to make you feel justified in banning them, but continually pushing your boundaries and making your channel feel uncomfortable, can be difficult to work out how to deal with. It's not like banning them is a clear solution anyway! They can still make new accounts, and so they lurk in the back of your head, and you find yourself thinking of them every time you see a new user in chat and notice they're behaving in a comparable way. Or they can follow you to other platforms, or go watch channels similar to yours, where they might feel free to spread negativity about you and tell others that they think you've treated them unfairly.

It feels like as your barriers get stronger, the ways in which manipulative viewers work shift accordingly. You're never quite rid of people who are trying to engineer ways to get your attention and emotional energy. When you stop people from messaging you directly to ask for emotional support, they start instead messaging you offering to do something for your community: "I'll make a database about your streams," "I'll make a soundtrack for your channel," things like that. Instead of reliably and continually delivering on these promises, you'll get a little bit of them, but then the actual reason that they reached out—a desire for your attention and familiarity with you—wins out, and they stop providing the service they said they'd do for you and start sending you more and more familiar messages. It feels impossible to tell who's going to follow through on their offer, and who is only in it for your attention. Reaching a point in my career where I could have Hannah find contractors to hire to complete whatever odd jobs I needed done was a massive boon for my stress levels.

Women, in particular, have endless stories about sexualization and inappropriate comments. Most of my friends hear so many iterations of "you're beautiful" and "I could make you feel like a real woman" that they begin to consider it a normal part of work. Hannah tried streaming for a while; after the first couple of weeks, we had a conversation where she kept on talking around something she'd been struggling with, speaking vaguely about "bad behavior," and I said, "You're being sexually harassed at work, and it isn't okay." She audibly exhaled and agreed.

After I asked for stressful examples from streaming, a few of the women I know shared specific incidents that had stuck with them. I've had people express that they'd like to hurt me before, but never with details, and I felt awful when my friends shared experiences where men had messaged them their previous address and told them they were going to slit their throat, or—in a comment that I'm very close to too uncomfortable to share— "fuck [them] with a knife."

A lot of viewers don't understand this, and when I'm asked what my favorite restaurant in Seattle is, or whether I'd like help from someone's wife to find an apartment, I try to delicately explain that I do not want to give away information about my private life without sharing the full force of why that is important for me to avoid. One streamer friend shared a story about four random people who knocked on his door on an otherwise unremarkable Wednesday night and, when he answered, said, "We found you!" I find myself wondering how many people who hear that story understand just how terrifying it is.

If it feels like we've veered into the most extreme cases here, I'd guess more than 90% of professional streamers have personal experience with harassment like this. But at least the harassment isn't a daily occurrence for most of us.[20] These do come daily: constant boundary-setting and adapting to being what someone else wants you to be, and dealing with a *lot* of entitlement and overfamiliarity.

Imagine setting a world record in a game which has sold 1.5 million copies—all the stress, difficulty, practice, pain, and emotion that goes into achieving that. Now imagine doing so while three thousand people watch, many of them treating you with the same lack of respect that they'd cruelly show to a server at a restaurant or a checkout person at a grocery store, and you start to understand what's going on. A lot of people see part of it—that you're playing a game, or that you're in front of lots of people, or that you're putting up with lots of demands—and think it must not be all that hard because they don't see that the rest of it is happening at the same time.

And so people will say, "I answer phones for a company, and people are rude to me all the time. It isn't such a big deal." They miss that it's more like answering calls while three thousand people watch them on a webcam feed, and they try to answer more calls in a day than anyone else in the history of humanity, and the people on the other end of the line know their real name and who their friends are.

---

20 For the unfortunate few of us for whom it is, law enforcement turns out to be comically incapable of serving and enforcing a restraining order on someone from another state or country whom you've never even technically met.

It's hard to say whether having more viewers makes it all better or worse. On the one hand, every additional viewer is another potential fire to put out, but on the other hand, a larger paycheck and more experience both go a long way toward managing those fires. I like to say that I have an ego like a lacrosse ball; appropriately sized, such that it'll bounce off walls without changing shape and spring back if someone pokes it. I started streaming with an ego more like unfired clay, which would collapse when pressed on by someone else. And any time my ego has started to resemble a balloon—over-sized such that it starts to be full of air—the Internet has quickly deflated or popped it. I'm certain that I couldn't have handled any of this as well as I have if I'd been thirteen when my channel took off.

Anyway. In spite of the downsides, it's a good job. I love it. The rewards when it goes well are astonishing, and I can't imagine wanting to do anything else.

It's hard, though, and I think sometimes that miserable treatment from the worst viewers makes it harder for streamers to expect and demand respectful treatment from our sponsors and managers—and even our friends and partners—all of whom can sometimes be just as eager to disrespect and hurt us, and who sometimes have much more real power over our lives.

TWIN FALLS

The only piece of theatre I've ever truly hated was a student play I went to in Manhattan while visiting a friend.

We were sitting in a small room. The actors were walking in amongst the crowd to truly immerse us in their performance. But the story was unremarkable, and I remember feeling trapped and miserable as a young actor delivered a lengthy monologue about watching an escalator descend in a subway and seeing in it all of the natural beauty of a waterfall.

I am still unable to reconcile the monologue with any sort of reality. Sometimes I wonder if the actor and playwright had simply never seen a waterfall. Or maybe they intended some deep irony which I wasn't privy to—the entire performance seemed incredibly earnest.

The earnestness with which someone can pretend—even believe—that something which is fake is real, or that something artificial is natural, was on my mind as I sat on a couch in the middle of Tyson Ranch in Los Angeles. F2K seemed to be moving up in the world in 2019, and this long weekend—when a bunch of us flew out to meet Mike Tyson and talk about his promised investment in our company—was the epitome of that success. I was working during the first half of the weekend but flew down for the last two days to hang out at the Ranch and meet a lot of the members of the team in person for the first time, along with its new sponsors.

If the name "Tyson Ranch" evokes beautiful imagery of native plants and horses, the actual experience missed that mark. We were in a medium-sized single-story rectangular building in El

Segundo with an open floor plan and a few offices and meeting rooms. In theory it was near the ocean, but in practice it was near a 7-11. The legal team interrupted a conversation about creating a streaming house here by pointing out that Mike was a convicted sex offender and shouldn't have young women living in a house he was paying for. None of it struck me as particularly genuine, useful, or impressive.

I had arrived in LA without even knowing the address of the house where we were staying. I love traveling if I'm in the mood for it. Days of international flights between New Zealand and the United States as a child taught me to turn my brain off and give myself over to the monotonous experience of airplanes and airports. It always feels a bit like going home. I hadn't planned to travel down from Seattle at all, but I had seen how much fun everyone seemed to be having and decided I might as well, so I walked out my front door and headed to the airport.

I got the address from a text when I arrived at LAX and grabbed an Uber to a house on the Marina Del Rey Peninsula. It was fancy, a couple of minutes' walk from the beach.

The outside table was covered in cigarette butts and empty beer cans. The front door was ajar and the inside looked like the aftermath of a college party. Nobody seemed to be around until I called out that I was there and John poked his head over the balcony from upstairs.

I started instinctually tidying the place up out of a sense of awkward shame, and John joined me. I did quite a lot of tidying up that weekend. We chatted about my flight and how the weekend had been going so far. Almost all of the team was already at Tyson Ranch; here it was just John and a young woman I'd never met.

They were both from Europe, and he had decided to fly her out for the weekend so that they could meet. Later, I heard weird rumors about this. When I asked her about it directly,[21] a couple of years afterward, she said she hadn't realized what was going on until other people told her that John had a thing for her. She said he had never tried anything or touched her inappropriately, and that she still considered him a friend and got help from him for her stream. She said that she felt other people might have taken advantage of her in those moments, but he didn't, and she really appreciated that.

It was a weird conversation. She was telling me it wasn't a big deal, but I wanted her to be screaming at me about how it was awful. I was expecting her to say something like "Yes, obviously it's wrong for the CEO of the team you contract for, who is ten years older than you, to use company funds to pay for you to fly internationally for a weekend to meet him because he has a crush on you."

Some women would be willing to say that, and their opinions might go viral on social media as they talked about an awful interaction they had with someone, but others wouldn't, and my impression is that I mostly don't hear about them. The sight of Lady Retribution is narrow. When the #MeToo movement hit streaming, groups of women joined voices to call out bad actors in the space, and it was wonderful to see. But that only happened in the places which had enough women to band together, and only when those women were brave and angry enough to speak out. Friends I talk to who work as solo women in gaming companies express how shallow the purge was, and tell me about men who have escaped all blame, or who were rightly

---

21 Working out whether it was worth it to initiate awful conversations to try to confirm rumors and tell this story as fully as possible was complicated. I felt primarily that I wanted to believe anything I was told, and didn't want to press anyone into unwillingly reliving past traumas. But at the same time, I wanted to make sure that everyone who wanted to contribute their voice was offered a chance to be heard.

accused of impropriety and then acquitted by internal company investigations, leaving everyone to pretend that nothing had ever happened.

It was also a weird conversation because, even though it wasn't a big deal to her, it was still awful for other people. John was in a long-term relationship with someone else at the time, and ended it by phone while I was there. He boasted to the guys back at work about this new girl he was connecting with. Other women on the team saw it happening and were grossed out. I saw what was happening and was grossed out. One evening, the two of them got an Uber back to the house before anyone else. John asked me if I wanted to come too, since I wasn't doing anything at the Ranch anymore, while very heavily implying that I should say "no." I felt like I was being asked to endorse him making a move on this young woman on a work weekend while she was thousands of miles from her home.

I decided to stay at the Ranch, largely because I felt too awkward to do anything else. I still regret that decision. When I think about moments I've been exposed to inappropriate behavior and could have done something differently, it's one of the main instances that I remember. One of the ways people can manipulate you is to make you feel complicit in their bad behaviors by telling you what they're doing without offering you any easy ways to stop them. You wake up the next day, or week, or month, or year, and realize that you've been going along with something awful the entire time, and it gets progressively harder to say "No, this isn't me!" and stop it. But this time, there was a relatively easy thing I could have done, and I just failed to do it.

On the morning I arrived, I didn't know about any of this—yet. It was a little weird that the two of them had been alone in the house together when I arrived, but I didn't think much of it. We took an Uber Plus to Tyson Ranch, and the driver, hearing that we were in the tech space, proceeded to talk our ears off about cryptocurrency. He was part of a group which was setting up crypto mining in some far-flung region of the world which was cold all the time, so they didn't have to pay as much for the electricity bill. Us two streamers checked out in the back seat while John cheerily engaged him on the subject.

John never stopped talking, ever. Not in the car ride, not anywhere else. I woke up to him talking and fell asleep to him talking. I spent five minutes in the bathroom once, and he checked in with me through the door.

I spent a while wondering why someone who was getting rich off crypto would be driving an Uber on the weekend. Maybe he actually was rich and just wanted people to hang out with. Maybe he wanted to make a few extra bucks to invest even more. Many people who were investing in crypto in 2019 were genuinely getting wealthy.

We arrived at the Ranch, and I waited outside the car while the driver pitched John an opportunity to invest in the mining group, which he turned down. After typing in the code on the keypad outside, we walked into the big, open space. The team was scattered throughout a variety of offices, running streams with each other. A few were chilling out in the central space on the couches.

Over that weekend, I would spend a lot of time chatting with John. I'd still only been on the team for six months, and this was the first time we'd met in person. He was one of the people I connected with most easily on the team, and he was doing the things I found most interesting: talking with investors, strategizing about the company, and meeting other streamers from LA to chat about the industry with them. Edison Park of OfflineTV stopped by, and the three of us chatted for a few hours about how to create successful streaming relationships.

John had a simple rhythm to him. Every four hours or so he would step outside for a cigarette and an energy bar. He would pick one or two people to go outside with him so he had someone to talk to. The rest of the time, he was inside talking with people. It was the hardest I had ever seen someone work in my life. I came away with the impression that he was at least slightly crazy but that it might be one of the good kinds to have working with you. I didn't have a lot of experience to judge this stuff on yet.

***

Do you ever watch popping videos? They're truly disgusting—I am sorry to have brought them up. But they do quite well on TikTok and YouTube; they're directly adjacent to the space I work in. You load up a video and watch a beautician squeeze out blackheads and other types of skin monsters, perhaps with some relaxing music playing in the background—or, on one popular channel, a voiceover recounting the narrator's experience of making the video, where she is, for example, squeezing what she believes to be decades of deodorant buildup out of pores in a woman's armpit. Sometimes I load up a popping video in the evening to wind down. I don't know why. I have a chronic skin condition, so maybe I find it comforting to see that other people have gross skin, too. Maybe I'm just gross in general. Or maybe this is how all of us are, and there isn't actually anything gross about it at all.

There is something logical and calming about a beautician removing someone's blackheads. The good ones have mastered techniques which achieve this with minimal damage to the skin around the pore. Some of them do almost comical showmanship, holding the corruptive demon goop which they have expunged from someone's face, or ear, or back, in front of the camera to impress upon the viewer that it is . . . big? Gross? *Beautiful?*

But outside this sterilized medical space, which was already pretty awful to witness,[22] even more awful are the homemade videos of explosive zits, boils, and cysts. I usually skip over these, and if I ever do watch them, my face glazes over in abject horror. My ex-partner used to come over to watch with me and agree that, yeah, what we'd just seen was vile. I introduced these videos to her as an awful thing we should absolutely not watch, and then she got really into them and validated my transgression. I used to jokingly blame her for all this.

Homemade videos where people, often lively characters slurring their speech from alcohol consumption, set up with a needle and poke some pure evil lump which has been growing on their friend's back for the last four years, and then squeeze really hard, and start screaming when the bile of Satan blossoms like napalm across the room—or, in some particularly fortuitous and unsettling situations, straight at the camera lens—are usually quite a bit too much for me.

The fact that these videos exist at all should probably trouble us more than it does. It isn't that there's anything evil about them; acne is taboo to many people, but it's an unnecessary taboo, perhaps a holdover from a time with different hygiene standards, which does little in the modern era other than to attack the self-esteem of people with otherwise harmless skin conditions.

The problem isn't that pimple-popping is a taboo; it's that a taboo of any sort can find a receptive community on the Internet. The thing is, the Internet doesn't know whether a topic of interest is good or evil. It doesn't care or judge. It just knows that a lot of people are fascinated by and drawn to this taboo, and provides a place for them to partake in it together. It isn't the pimples that are gross; it's the mechanism that allows thousands of people to

---

22 Sometimes my mouth begins filling with saliva as I watch a video, which I'm pretty sure is my body priming itself to vomit. I have no ability to explain why I continue watching these.

watch these videos together. Because the same mechanism allows thousands of sexist people to watch sexist videos, or racist people to watch racist videos, and the Internet is just as eager to enable that behavior. *That's* something which is truly disgusting.

I found myself thinking of pimples, of those vile sprays of putrescence, one afternoon a couple of years later, after I'd been talking to Hannah about this weekend in Los Angeles. She hadn't come—she'd rejoined F2K later in 2019, but that summer she was still at her warehouse job—but she'd heard stories from John, and from some of the other staff and streamers when she came back to the team. I was working on the second draft of this book, trying to introduce more structure and make sure that the story followed a main thread, and it was forcing me to ask people questions about things which I'd skipped over on the first write because I didn't really want to know the answers. So, I asked her whether her personal relationship with John was something we should talk about. Hannah and I were close enough friends by this point that it felt okay to be asking. I think she'd known the question was coming for a while.

It was an open secret that John had a thing for Hannah. I don't know when it started exactly—maybe it's the reason she was hired as his personal assistant after her position as a tournament admin closed. I'd heard it from other people, I'd heard it from Hannah, and I'd heard it from John himself. It was also obvious that she had a great deal of respect and affection for him. And so it seemed like I should ask what happened there. She said, "I entertained the notion, then I noticed a lot of red flags, and I realized that I would not be happy with someone like him." I asked her what the red flags were, and it was like squeezing at exactly the right angle. The four-year-old boil erupted, a violent waterfall of disgust.

She talked for five minutes nonstop. I interjected small things like "Jesus, Hannah" and "fuuuuuck" but otherwise just listened to what she had to say. She said that she'd started to notice that things John said weren't always true—he was "back and forth" with the things he would say to her. He had a neurotic obsession with the Red Pill YouTube channel and told her that *The 48 Laws of Power* was his Bible.[23] He'd joked that his staff were slaves, and she'd heard him and Cody discussing how they could make other people "work for pennies."

She said she didn't like how he and another male staff member would link each other women's Twitch channels and talk about how they were going to blow up "because they were hot." He used that and other "locker room" talk[24] while she was there, hearing it all, and she felt pressured to act like it was okay or she'd be left out of the loop on important company decisions because she wasn't "cool." She said she put up with it to survive, and to move up the company ladder at F2K. John had promised her that she'd be chief of operations, so she went along with it all so she could "be something." Eventually she got to the point where she was sitting in meetings and staying silent the entire time as she listened to the other staff members objectify women streamers. John showed her his awful behavior in a way which she was powerless to correct, and made her complicit.

She told me that John loved basing analogies about business on Tinder—I know about this from personal experience talking to him—and that it became a trigger for her, filling her with disgust. She'd sit in meetings, and men would make comments like, "Hannah is the kind of girl you'd swipe right for." When John found himself single and started looking for a new girlfriend, she

---

23 The book's blurb on Amazon: "Amoral, cunning, ruthless, and instructive, this multi-million-copy *New York Times* bestseller is the definitive manual for anyone interested in gaining, observing, or defending against ultimate control."

24 Throughout my life, I have made it very clear that I'm not okay with talking about women like this in locker rooms.

said he'd sent shirtless pictures of himself to her and some of the women on the team, asking if they'd be good Tinder profile pics.

None of this is surprising to me, really. John had said stuff like this to me, too, and I was uncomfortable about it myself. One day he was talking about how he'd used a site to get ratings for his Tinder profile pics, and had matched with a girl who was a "perfect 10." I grimaced and tried to explain to him that this did not sound like a great start to a healthy relationship. I gave him some feedback on how my idea of a relationship worked: That myself and my partner had mutual respect for each other, were honest about what we were looking for when we met, and that I certainly didn't go around boasting about how great I thought she was as a personal sex object.

I definitely didn't get through. He and his "perfect 10" ended up dating long-term, and John continued to break professional boundaries by leaning on me for relationship advice and support whenever things weren't going how he would've liked. I developed stress responses to John's requests to talk because he never told me what he wanted to talk about; I'd have no idea whether he wanted to tell me about a new sponsor, or he was firing me, or he was upset with someone, or he needed to vent. Because John refused to make healthy boundaries between his personal and professional lives, I felt that disagreeing with any of his personal behavior risked repercussions for my professional success.

LOVE AND FRIENDSHIP

Relationship abuse often hides behind closed doors, especially lower-intensity relationship abuse—the stuff without bruise marks and which isn't loud enough to wake the neighbors. In April 2011, I lost my ability to play poker online in the United States, and while I was processing the idea that I was now functionally unemployed, my girlfriend of five years got the news that her mother had been given a terminal cancer diagnosis. I had been living in LA while she finished school, and decided I had to stick around and give whatever support I could—which turned out to be completely insignificant and insufficient for this sort of situation. My ex started abusively taking all of her stress out on me, and I had almost nothing in the city to help me stand up to her—no family, few friends, and no job.

Meanwhile, her mother fought on. A completely indomitable woman, she was given six months to live and, two years later, managed to out-survive our relationship after my ex finally ended it by essentially starting to date someone else while we were still living together.

I'd thought the calculus was fairly clear. I could tell it was relationship abuse. I knew where it was coming from—her father had been physically abusive, and her parents had gone through a bad divorce which had defined a lot of her adolescence. She didn't deal with emotions well, and her mother was dying down the street. At the time, I rationalized that I was strong enough to survive it and that she loved me and needed my support. I now know that I was *not* that strong, and that I was an idiot.

For two years, I was told almost every day by the person I loved more than anything else in the world that I was worthless, lazy, unattractive; that I lacked confidence; that I could never lead anyone; and, more generally, that this was because I was a man, and all men were terrible. The abuse stayed mostly verbal and emotional, but on particularly bad days she would also throw things at me, and on the worst night I actually felt physically endangered and barricaded myself in our bedroom. She spent fifteen minutes trying to break the door down by ramming it with her shoulder, and then called the police and told them I was locking her out of her own bedroom. When they arrived, I finally felt safe to come out again, and one of the officers asked me if I had been hurting her ("What? I would never hurt her!") and then warned me that, if this went to court, judges and juries were likely to side with the woman.

If you're in an abusive relationship and you can leave it, leave it. If you're in an abusive relationship and you can't leave it, leave it anyway. It happens rarely—I love to overthink anything and everything—but sometimes I do believe that simple rules are the right rules.

After I got dumped, I called my mother to tell her that I was completely alone and jobless in Los Angeles, and had spent the last week sitting in a chair and drinking. She told dad and he took a long weekend to drive down from Seattle, help me load my stuff into a trailer, and drive me back up to Seattle again. I spent three years or so trying to stitch myself back together again. I lived off poker earnings and played a lot of *League of Legends* in my parents' basement. I lost a lot of friends—one time, someone shared a satirical article about manspreading on Facebook, and I lost two nights of sleep and ended two friendships over it. I couldn't detach criticism of male behavior from the way my ex had dragged my identity down into the mud for two years of my life. Since then, my relationships have tended to end after it becomes problematic that half of the things in my body related to sex and attachment still don't work properly or at all due to the psychological effects of said abuse.[25] In her kinder moments, my abuser would tell me that I'd do well with women after she dumped me, and I would protest that I didn't want to be with other women because she was the one for me. We were mostly both wrong. I do fine with women and want to be with them, but I'll probably never fully love someone again. Maybe someday. I pay for a lot of therapy. I loved my most recent partner, as much as I could, but she spent a lot of time frustrated at sharing her life with (in my opinion) about half of a person.[26]

It would be easy to discard the relationship abuse as a wholly negative experience, but one good thing did come out of it: I became completely disillusioned with the idea that I knew how to interact with women. In fact, after it was over, I couldn't hear or read the words "man" or "woman" without having a minor meltdown. My heart would start pounding, my teeth would clench, and I'd start thinking about all the ways in which gender was evil and hurtful. And so I reinvented the way I made new friendships and relationships, basically from first principles, like I might have in a game, and it made me realize that I could use the skills I'd learned in gaming for different goals. After a childhood

---

25 I can't remember what arousal used to feel like, but ever since that relationship it has felt like my heart has dropped three inches lower in my chest and I can't breathe.

26 The way I think about attachment these days is: it's like a muscle which is overly tight for me. I *want* to be able to sit cross-legged, or whatever other thing you'd like to use as a metaphor for good attachment, but to succeed I have to stretch for hours a day, and it is tiring and difficult for me to do that, especially since I've traumatically injured this muscle before. And so I struggle to feel properly close to anyone, and my brain and body struggle to properly understand why that is, and I find myself wishfully imagining meeting someone I can simply click with and easily love, like I used to be able to do when I was twenty.

in gaming circles where women almost didn't exist, this abusive relationship was the experience which catalyzed my examining the ways I thought about and interacted with gender, and after three years of listening and reading and introspection I arrived at ground-breaking ideas like "women are people" and "they are mostly just like me, but their actions respond to the world treating them very differently from how it treats me." These are ideas which still escape many men who were raised in male-dominated strategy gaming circles.[27]

One of the reasons Hannah left F2K after I joined the team in the beginning of 2019 was that she was going through some relationship struggles of her own. She ended up breaking up with her ex, Jake, that summer. They're still close friends and support each other in ways that I think are beautiful, but they had come to terms with the fact that their romance was over. A few months after she'd left the team—after her demotion from COO—she came back and took a lower-responsibility position, managing some of the streamers. Soon afterward, I heard from her that she had been talking to another streamer I knew, and they'd hit it off. They were getting *romantically involved*. I was excited for them; I'm genuinely excited for anybody who manages the optimism and trust required to be happy and eager about a relationship.

A couple of months later, she shared with me that the new relationship wasn't living up to expectations. She had started dating this streamer because he made her laugh and feel cared

---

27 This is a somewhat biting turn of phrase, and a few readers have commented "you should make sure that it's clear to your audience that you're exaggerating to be funny, here." So, I feel obliged to clarify that I am not exaggerating. I've met men who, despite being able to compete with the best in the world at complex strategy games, don't understand either of those things about women. And some of them were role models for me, growing up, so it genuinely took me a while to understand that properly, as well.

for, but now he was putting her down and trying to control her. My relationship abuse sirens started blaring.

Online streaming spaces are riddled with women who have incredibly strong boundaries in place because their inbound messages fill up with literal and metaphorical dick pics any time they make themselves available for conversation. Imagine catcalling, except in a context where the woman deliberately tries to look good all the time, with good lighting, and there are two thousand men watching at the same time, all of whom are able to be completely anonymous. And that's just with regard to viewers. What about the CEO of a team you want to join who invites you out to dinner? The community manager for the game you play who asks if you'd like to continue your conversation about participating in their official tournaments over drinks? What if someone wants to fly you to LA to introduce you to Mike Tyson?

Consent in the streaming space can feel very cloudy. If a guy with a channel fifty times larger than yours and a history of making or breaking other streamers based on his approval asks you out on a date, are you really getting to freely decide between yes or no? The same question hovers when a streamer asks out a talent manager. I don't know the answers for these ones.

When I started streaming, I burned out on the first two main games I played almost completely because I couldn't handle their communities. They were both small games—*XCOM* and *Faster Than Light*—and I was very good at them, but I didn't like some of the other streamers in the communities, didn't like the way the communities talked about my content, and didn't understand how to navigate those relationships. So, I left *XCOM* to try *FTL*, then left *FTL* to try another game, and eventually, with a bit of trial and error, I got to a place where I could play a game, become known in the community, and not feel constantly overwhelmed and stressed out by what the community around the game was like.

While finding a healthy place to carve out a community was challenging for me, women have this significantly worse than men. For starters, they aren't given anywhere near as much credit for their skills, and have to work a lot harder to earn their place in a community. My friend Hafu has been a figurehead of women in gaming for over a decade, but to get there, she had to get past attending a *World of Warcraft* regionals tournament at age seventeen, where one of her team's rivals was named "Gonna Rape Hafu at Regionals." How they were not automatically disqualified for choosing a name like this is completely unfathomable to me.[28]

Nicholena, a hero of mine and a role model for women in gaming, has been succeeding at card games at a competitive level for more than a decade. She started out playing the Pokémon Trading Card Game, but nowadays she streams *Hearthstone*. She speaks openly and adamantly about sexism both in and out of the *Hearthstone* community. In 2019, she finally got a nod and was invited to a live event by Blizzard.

I asked her about that event, and when I mentioned hearing that the *Hearthstone* community manager had hit on her while she was there, she said she thought that phrasing was too strong. At the same time, she wondered if that had been intentional— maybe he'd wanted it to seem unclear, so that he couldn't be held accountable later. His work emails to her had heart emojis in them. At the event, he'd done things like sending her his SoundCloud, sitting a bit too close one time and asking to see all

---

28 Twelve years later, in 2022, Activision Blizzard paid $18 million to settle an unrelated sexual harassment lawsuit brought against them. The company was valued at $70 billion at the time, and to my knowledge that was the first time that they had been punished in any way for their continued toxic workplace environment. I doubt there were any women in the company in position to have oversight over Hafu's tournament, despite its competitors including at least one seventeen-year-old girl.

her tattoos, and messaging an invitation to hang out with him at 2 a.m. She declined.

After that, she stopped getting invited to events. The next event had seven out of eight of the same people, but she saw that her slot had been taken by a different woman. Blizzard even stopped including her in promotions and giveaways, and she spent a year and a half seeing other streamers promoted and validated by the company, while she was ignored. She didn't understand why this was happening. Would things have been different if she'd agreed to hang out with him, or tried to impress him? Was she just not friendly enough? She wondered if maybe they had only needed one or two women and had chosen someone more conventionally attractive and clean-cut than her.

The first time she was passed over for an event, she asked the community manager if she'd done something wrong and was told that she hadn't. She felt better for a bit, but then she kept getting excluded. The next time he told her that she hadn't done anything wrong, she didn't accept it, and pushed back on his claim that he was "spreading the love around." (As an outside observer, I find the claim hilarious. *Hearthstone* invitationals and giveaways have had an incredibly predictable cast of six or so of the same ten men and one or two women for the entire time I've followed the game.) She argued for inclusion of more streamers, especially women and people of color, and he became heated and indignant. He stopped giving excuses and told her that she was "entitled" and that he didn't work with content creators "like her." She felt like she was being misunderstood, and tried to explain that she loved the game, and all she was trying to do was advocate for more inclusion. He blocked her on social media.

A year or so passed, and other stories came out, and she decided it was time to speak up. In the most electric stream I've ever watched, she spent an evening talking about sexism and discrimination in gaming, sharing stories of her own and of her friends. Her chat was exploding, with other women in the community hosting her channel and staying to watch and support her. Blizzard heard, and the community manager got on a call with her again and apologized to her, saying that he recognized that Blizzard had hurt her growth and career. She felt frustrated and gaslit. She asked why she was blacklisted and was told that she had "leaked something," but wasn't provided any evidence of what it was. When she asked why he'd blocked her, he said that it was for "personal reasons." She felt like he had been coached by a lawyer.

Even if women are good at a game, and become recognized as good, and get invited to play, what happens next? After Pathra reached #2 rank on the North American server[29] and ended multiple seasons in the top 100 on the leaderboards, she was invited to play in *Hearthstone* Grandmasters, an officially sanctioned tournament circuit for the game.

After her invite, instead of getting a fair chance to prove herself, Pathra became a target for harassment. She was the only "girl." Viewers bombarded her with hatred and derision any time she made a mistake—mistakes which would have been criticized more analytically if made by a man. Just her introduction on the tournament's broadcast led to waves of misogynistic and cruel messages being posted in the channel's chat—messages like "Why

---

29   She only ever claims she reached #4, which is the rank she reached playing completely on her own. When she reached #2 it was with a friend on call with her and they were talking through plays together, and a lot of the competitive grinders of the game have framed this as meaning that her friend was the one who was "actually" good. But she reached #4 on her own, so she's obviously incredibly good. And every man in the space would happily claim that #2 placement, even if he was on a call with a friend when he achieved it. I'm going to say she reached #2, because she did.

am I watching a girl?" or "I'd rather watch Kibler's dog[30] than Pathra", which weren't deleted by moderators—Blizzard didn't have chat moderators at all for the year she was on the circuit. She knew it was happening, even if she didn't look, and struggled to focus on her games. Many members of her community, wanting to support her, found that they couldn't stand watching the broadcast with the chat open, and some of them found they couldn't handle watching it at all.

She had trouble finding anyone to practice with—far from wanting to collaborate with her, some of the other competitors were in a public Discord server talking interchangeably about how bad they thought she was and whether or not she was as hot as the other women who played the game.[31] Members of her community stepped up, and she tested with a couple of her moderators, while a viewer went over decks with her. Checking social media had been stressful for me when a few people were sharing fair criticisms of my content. For her, social media was full-blown bullying and sexual harassment, sometimes from her co-competitors, and it was leaking into her direct messages and personal channel, where she couldn't choose to ignore it. While F2K wasn't great to me, I at least felt like I was clearly on the team on merit, and felt validated and empowered when I received the invitation. In comparison, Pathra once told me that she'd found out after a few months on her first esports

---

30 Referring to Brian Kibler's loveable Pomeranian, Shiro, who, in my opinion, would have bitten these people's ankles if he had understood what was going on.

31 The Discord's owner encouraged the harassment, framing Pathra's invite to the tournament circuit as her taking a place in the circuit that he deserved. She was stunned when, despite the lengthy history of harassment, he hit on her at a live event she was invited to, repeatedly asking her to let him come back to her hotel room with her. After she turned him down, she got home from the event and found that he had started harassing her even more.

team that she had been signed because one of the men on staff wanted a chance to hit on her.

I can't imagine it. Every woman I have met who has survived in the strategy gaming segments of this industry is an impervious juggernaut of a human being—and often, even they are only holding on by threads. I have seen the best minds of my generation having panic attacks in the backs of convention centers. Those who persevere develop incredible coping mechanisms—my friend Emma tells me about how she and her partner play "dick pic or not?" with incoming messages on Instagram, and when she talks about a continued trend of harassment targeting her with pictures comparing her face to a horse's on social media, she laughs and says "I like horses!"[32]

Since women in gaming receive so much treatment which is horrible, yet normalized and endemic, I felt like it would be easy for a woman in this space to be especially vulnerable to relationship abuse. It reminded me of how I'd lived in Los Angeles: alone, with few friends and no family, and no secure source of income. I'd felt vulnerable and powerless when someone chose to prey on me. So when Hannah told me that her relationship wasn't living up to what she'd signed on for anymore, I was terrified.

I knew the streamer she was involved with professionally. He was a smart guy, he made funny jokes, and he was powerfully and successfully logical. I wasn't all that surprised to find out he was also broken, though. Processing human beings into viewer metrics and subscription or advertising revenue borders on psychopathy, even without the other context.

---

32 It feels gross to mention this, because it shouldn't matter—no one should be bullied for their appearance, no matter how they look—but Emma made the quarterfinals of a competition to be a cover model for Maxim. The harassment these women receive isn't targeted at any relevant trait that they actually have, such that a perfect human might be spared from it; it's targeted at the fact that they are women.

I think the most brutal and vulnerable way of summarizing the toxic masculinity in strategy gaming is that boys who play strategy games are often the kids who got beat up in school, and they want to beat other people up in an arena that they control as a misguided attempt to reclaim their masculinity. Slightly more gently: It's a place where people who suffer from trauma go, because they can grapple with danger in a place which is safe and under their control. I wasn't physically bullied often as a kid, but I was certainly an outsider,[33] and I measured a lot of my self-worth as a teenager and young adult by whether or not I could beat other people at *Magic: The Gathering* and poker. I grew out of it, but it took a lot of time and work.

Gamers like to romanticize this: The thrill of matching wits against a worthy opponent. The extreme emotions of battle. The nervousness before a tournament and exhilaration (or frustration) at their results. The delicate dance along the threshold of death. I think it's all bullshit. They're all just looking for a way to prove that they're worth something, that they can tame this beast—whether it's chess or *League of Legends* or their opponent—and if you're comfortable in your self-worth, the competition elements of strategy gaming are mostly boring and smelly. I was carried away with the idea of competing against the best in the world at *Magic: The Gathering* once upon a time, but when I actually attended the World Championships in San Francisco (as a spectator), I realized pretty quickly that it was just a large rectangular convention hall with a bunch of plastic tables and body odor.

In *All the Wrong Moves*, Sasha Chapin refers tragically to his experience of making a pilgrimage to India to compete in a chess tournament only to get horribly sick and alternate between the hospital and the chess boards, where he found himself losing

---

33 My advice: Don't move internationally in middle school.

to eight-year-olds. A recent satirical Onion article hit the mark well, examining a thirty-five-year-old's struggle to understand why he was underwhelmed after earning first place in a *Magic: The Gathering* tournament. I spent years of my life searching for meaning which just wasn't there, before I finally realized that encouraging and empowering others to enjoy games was a much more meaningful achievement than winning at them.

The fixation on winning—sometimes to the point of cheating—is bizarre, unhealthy, and widespread. In early 2021 in the *Trackmania* community, a massive scandal exploded between the game's two largest content creators, Riolu and Wirtual. Riolu banned mentioning Wirtual in his channel's chat, and then went live one day and explained that he had been getting messages from Wirtual accusing him of cheating, and showed the evidence that he claimed had been provided: a single race Riolu had played about ten years ago where his control inputs looked inhuman. The community fractured, with thousands of Riolu's fans telling Wirtual that he shouldn't be making this kind of accusation.

I'm ashamed to say that I was one of them, suggesting to Wirtual that, even if Riolu had cheated in this one run from ten years ago, that was a long time ago, and it was better to just let sleeping dogs lie. I don't think any of us understood the level of manipulation that Riolu was capable of. When Wirtual's report was actually published, it contained infallible evidence that Riolu had cheated in over a thousand world record runs played over the course of the last ten years, leading up to a few months prior. The report also accused many other players of cheating with the same or similar methods, but on far fewer races, and almost all of them admitted their wrongdoing. Riolu disappeared completely, and as of the publication of this book hasn't streamed or posted anything publicly since the report came out. This person had once been watched by thousands of people, and recommended by many, including myself.

I had my own brush with cheating when a streamer openly lied to the *Slay the Spire* community about a win streak. He claimed to have won eight runs in a row at the highest difficulty at the time, tying one of my world records, and I was excited to check out his runs, so I skimmed through them on my phone on the way to an evening event. He was abusing a feature of the game to reload at the beginning of fights over and over again until he found the best way to play them in all of his runs, which is absolutely fine if you are just playing on your own, but absolutely cheating if you are then going to claim to the community that you have set a world record.

I could perhaps have interpreted that as simply being a misunderstanding of the communally-understood rules of win streaks, had he not also lost a run in the middle and told his (several hundred!) viewers that it just didn't count. I was pissed off that he had wasted my time and ruined my mood for the evening. I didn't have the patience and maturity of Wirtual, who painstakingly put together a report on cheating in *Trackmania*, then privately reached out to the parties accused to give them chances to admit their wrongdoings on their own terms. Instead, I called him out on what he'd done publicly and then banned him from chatting in my channel when he showed up in the middle of my livestream the next day to start arguing about it. In the three years since, I have been incredibly happy to ignore his existence; I just don't have any reason to care about him at all anymore. Meanwhile, he has sent me messages asking to be unbanned or asking for explanations for why he is banned, sent my moderators messages asking to be unbanned (some of them watch him too, so he managed to get unbanned once, forcing me to explain to all of my moderators why he was banned in the first place), and even made at least one new account to chat with in my channel and get around the ban.

He sent me a message on New Year's Eve one year saying that he wanted to make a fresh start with me, and I sent him back a polite attempt to say, "No, cheating on a world record and then harassing me for pointing it out is not something I'm going to forgive." Sometimes bridges burn and it isn't worth trying to rebuild them, and that feels especially true when you're already trying to cater to a hundred thousand other people.

All things considered, when a strategy game streamer turns out to be broken in some way, it isn't much of a surprise to me.

Still though, even if it isn't a surprise anymore, some of my most disturbed moments as a streamer have been finding out that someone I've recommended to my audience is awful. I woke up one day and saw that a streamer I'd supported had been credibly accused of sexual assault by three different women. And when you find out something horrible about someone, there's still no easy escape from these relationships. If you had a friend who behaved awfully, you'd presumably end the friendship, or at least you'd have enough agency to hang out with them less. In contrast, if another streamer in your ecosystem starts to get on your nerves, you have little ability to escape being asked about them twenty times a day by random people, every day of your life. It dampens the mood of an entertainment broadcast to repeatedly tell an audience of two thousand people, "Yeah, he got accused of sexual assault by three different women I trust, so I don't play *Stardew Valley* with him anymore." Plus, sometimes someone entrusts you with information about someone which they don't want you to speak about publicly at all. What are you meant to say then, exactly?

I eventually solved this by establishing that I didn't want anyone talking about other streamers on my channel except for me. It just wasn't reasonable or honest anymore. I couldn't say anything negative about anyone else, because it would spread as drama and awfulness to them and others, but if I couldn't say negative things about people, then I couldn't speak honestly about them. If a viewer asked me a question that I couldn't answer honestly, they weren't really asking me for an answer; they were asking me for a performance, and at some point I just decided I wasn't going to dress up for those requests. Performances are exhausting, and it feels dishonest to give them to someone who is expecting honesty.

The problem is that this is a cop-out. It means I'm never calling out bad behavior. It's one of the reasons that I've had a book trying to come out of my brain for the last few years, as I constantly suppress criticisms and warnings that I'd like to make about other people. It just isn't enough to have your best friend tell you that one of your colleagues is abusing her, and then go to work the next day and smile and tell a viewer asking a question about him, "I prefer not to answer questions about other streamers on this channel."

I eventually arrived at the "healthy" solution of avoiding interaction with streamers immediately adjacent to me as much as I possibly could. I have friends who are streamers—some of them quite good friends!—but they play other games and stream at other times of the day, and often my audience doesn't know much about our friendship. If I asked my viewers which streamers I'd talked to offline the most in the last week, none of them would get the top two right. If I stopped wanting to be friends with those streamers, none of my viewers would hear about it, because they wouldn't have known we were friends in the first place. And if I continue being friends with them, and our friendship becomes stronger, my viewers still probably won't know about it, because having friendships that double as pre-arranged public work relationships is fucking weird.

But lots of streamers don't have that option. They're clawing for relevance and struggling with boundaries and trying to force friendships with strangers whom they sort of work with (though they might not even have the same overall goals), and it often gets dramatic and bizarre. Affection misfires, emotions build up, things said privately don't match things said publicly. Sometimes beautiful friendships happen! Sometimes people get married! And sometimes you find out that someone who shares a huge chunk of your viewer base is abusing one of your friends.

SUPPORT

I never actually got to meet Mike Tyson, which I guess would have been sort of fun. My general impression of celebrities is that they're mostly completely normal people, but Mike was on another level of fame from anyone else I'd met. I hung out a little outside his podcast studio while he was getting high and recording a conversation with some other guy I probably should have recognized. Five or so members of their respective posses were chilling outside, passing a joint around. There was a lot of weed. Also various CBD products—I enjoyed a beverage that was a can of carbonated water with CBD oil in it. It tasted like carbonated water and left me feeling somewhat hydrated. One day I arrived at 8 a.m., and three of the guys were already in one of the offices sharing their different strains with each other. It was the only time I'd heard people talk about weed like they were wine snobs.

By far the most jarring experience I had at Tyson Ranch was with Harry, a member of Tyson's staff charged with handling the investment in F2K. John introduced me to him as F2K's biggest streamer (an exaggeration which clawed at being almost true) and set up a meeting with him and a few other members of Mike's staff to talk about their ideas for the team. So, I went from my tiny apartment in Seattle—where I usually sat on my own talking into a webcam and microphone—to a boardroom at Tyson Ranch, where suddenly I was speaking face to face with businessmen interested in throwing around tens of millions of dollars. Harry began the conversation by mentioning a lesson he'd learned while working with the founder of Napster, which was something else.

Name-dropping is a central part of Los Angeles culture—and by extension streaming culture—by which people attempt to establish their worth in an environment which has few sensible measures of worth. Basically, it's the scene from *American Psycho* where they have a dick-measuring contest over their business cards, except instead everyone competes to name the most impressive person that they knew ten years ago. In this exchange, I am usually a side character being offered the business card, confused about why it's being handed to me. The founder of Napster was a big step up from the caliber of namedrops I was used to, which tended to feature *Fortnite* streamers I hadn't heard of.

My usual response to these namedrops is confusion. There are basically three things that can happen:

1. I think the person being namedropped is genuinely impressive and wonder what on Earth you did wrong to end up working with me instead of them.

2. I've never heard of the person and have no reason to care about them.

3. More recently, sometimes I'm friends with them or we have a lot of mutuals, and I'm struck by the fact that you're mentioning them, but I've never heard them mention you.

But anyway, it was a power move. Harry mentioned Napster, and I was overwhelmed with memories of the time I'd downloaded an audio-only file of an *SNL* "Celebrity Jeopardy!" skit and the other high school freshmen thought I was cool for a couple of days. Maybe not the memory Harry meant to evoke, but in any case his alleged position as an elder statesman of online entertainment immediately gave him the upper hand in the conversation.

So. I was sitting across the table from Harry. John was in the chair next to me. Harry had an entire entourage, none of whom were introduced to me. Some guy at the head of the table had a laptop out with the screen facing away from everyone else, and he is the only person I've ever suspected was probably looking at pornography while at work. That was the general vibe I was getting from the group. A few other men positioned themselves around the room.

I walked into this conversation naively believing that Harry was interested in hearing my opinions about streaming and about how Mike's investment and resources could help us. But the conversation was never going to be about my opinions. John was trotting me out as a show horse, and because he wanted me to validate what he was doing for him. After I had spoken for a few minutes, Harry launched into a variety of anecdotes about his life which implied a massive misunderstanding of what F2K was, where it stood in the media landscape, and what projects it would make sense for it to focus on. I suddenly realized that I was talking to someone with no idea what was going on, but who was very used to being right, and who was surrounded by people who thought he knew what he was talking about.

The backend of streaming is incredibly unrefined. When a close friend who basically willed herself into a career on the management side of esports described the space to me, she said that she was impressed by end products, but constantly confused by individuals. She often felt, about certain men working in esports, that the only reason they'd been hired was that they'd been standing in the right place in 2012 when the major organizations were coming together. Even today, men are often hired because they know the right people, or have fancy qualifications in other spaces, rather than because they understand what's going on.

I've had plenty of my own experiences with men like this. The most egregious was Doug, whom I'd met when I first joined F2K. He was meant to help me build my YouTube channel, but instead introduced me to five different editors—none of whom ever made a watchable video I could publish—and spent hour-long calls avoiding my work questions by telling me tall tales about selling arms in Eastern Europe or dodging gang disputes in the urban sprawl of Los Angeles. Doug wasn't actually his name; he'd decided to use a regular first name for his online identity, and when questioned he straight-up told us that he didn't want to be referred to by his real name anymore because it carried too much negative baggage.

At some point I got frustrated enough at our lack of progress that I sent Doug a bulleted list of what I needed him to do for me before we were scheduled to get on a call together. He had a day to review this list and come up with a plan to help me with it before our call. He began the call by complimenting me on being so organized, then name-dropped a different content creator who was comparably organized (I hadn't heard of him) and spent the entire call talking about him while I desperately tried to redirect him to the issues I had raised. We never resolved a single thing on the list.

I soon gave up on getting anything done with Doug, and started treating the calls as social breaks. He was a conman, but he was so bad at it that it felt more like a show than a threat. I'd pour a glass of whisky or two and sit and listen as he talked nonstop about more and more unbelievable things. For a couple of months, I tried to tell John that Doug wasn't actually doing any work, but John either didn't care or didn't believe me.

Harry immediately reminded me of Doug—only with more authority and power. In fact, when Harry got more involved with F2K, the two of them became friends.

My friend—whose need to remain anonymous is a reminder of the amount of sexism frustratingly normalized in this industry—got her current job after reaching out to a female newcomer to the business to give her a list of guys in streaming and esports who were predators she'd need to avoid. These were men in positions of power, who never got mentioned in a MeToo movement, and who could end her career if she said the wrong thing. The guys who were merely incompetent, or flawed but harmless, didn't make it onto the list—it would be way too long.

My friend didn't hear back for a while; she figured the other woman probably thought she was overreacting. A couple of months later, she got a phone call from the woman, who had already seen enough of my friend's warnings validated to decide that she needed to hire her. Every month or so another massive scandal erupts—sort of like the pot is boiling and needs to let out steam—and when I see which man has been accused of awful behavior this time, I often find myself nodding and realizing I recognize his name from her list.

These men are not only predators toward women; their behavior is also directed at streamers more generally. The relationship between streamers and orgs is lopsided: Streamers are predominantly looking for reliability, validation, and social support—they want to be part of a team—while the orgs are looking to make money, and see the streamers as resources to be used to that end.

These fast-talking men can get away with saying just about anything they want about streaming, because there's little way for anyone to really know what works. A lot of success in the industry seems random, and there are few sensible cultural norms regarding behavior. This context easily leads to horribly abusive working environments, and repeatedly puts manipulative men into positions of power.

But in this conversation with Harry there was a fairly large elephant in the room: me. There are a few thousand people, maybe tens of thousands, who have achieved significant actual success in the streaming world, and they can tell fairly quickly if what you are saying has any relationship to a single thing they have ever seen succeed in the space. Harry's ideas did not. And further, among those people who can tell you're full of shit, there are a few who don't have enough social awareness to realize that they might be better off if they just played along and didn't say so. That's me. John wanted me to be his show horse, and sat next to me through the conversation—I think he expected me to be excited about it—but he forgot the blinders. I didn't need his shitty paycheck like Hannah did; I had sixty thousand or so followers on Twitch at this point, and they paid my rent regardless of my relationship with F2K. That meant I could stand up to people sometimes, and when someone sounded abusive to me, I was beginning to find that my vocal cords started moving.

Harry's main idea was to put together a first-person shooter team composed of typecast women which would compete in official tournaments and also create lifestyle content: the Spice Girls of video gaming. Where to start?

First off, a room full of men bankrolled by a convicted sex offender talking about typecasting women is transparently skeezy. Don't be skeezy.

Getting into the more complicated points now: Women have faced discrimination in gaming communities, including the first-person shooter community, for the entire existence of gaming. Very few exist who are good enough to compete professionally—not because men are favored innately over women in video gaming in any way, but because men and boys have been obnoxious assholes to women and girls who want to play video games for the last thirty years.[34] As a result, most of the women don't have ten years of playing five or more hours a day under their belts—which is pretty normal for male professionals in this space.

The idea of casting a team of streamers like this also didn't make any financial sense. Esports teams are loss-leaders. They try to build the team's brand, but there is no real way to make money off them. Player contracts get expensive, flying to tournaments is expensive, and practice facilities are expensive. Tournament prize pools aren't huge, and merch sales aren't enough. Given these realities, F2K's (semi-successful!) business model had historically been about negotiating deals for streamers who were already successful and profitable on their own, not fabricating some sort of team like this out of nowhere.

Even worse was the idea that the women would be slotted into typecast roles rather than simply streaming as themselves. Streaming should be about authenticity and honesty with your audience: The barriers between private and public break down. So instead of struggling to maintain a deceptive illusion eight hours a day for the rest of your life, risking completely losing your audience's trust at any moment, content creation is at its best when you can unleash vulnerable and real emotions on your audience.

Finally, a professional esports team would struggle to create lifestyle content while also being a professional team; they would

---

34   There is, of course, much more complexity to this than I managed to convey in my moment of righteous indignation with Harry. My friend Kyle once pointed out to me that she was never encouraged to play video games with her friends; it was culturally coded as an activity for boys. This underscored for me that it isn't enough just to be kind to women and girls who want to play games; I must also be accepting and encouraging, and never be judgmental of how they managed to find their way to the hobby, as the paths which were open to me were never available to many of them.

be busy competing! Get lifestyle content creators if you want to make lifestyle content.

My main instincts about the proposition were that it had no chance of ever being profitable or succeeding at anything other than making the women involved look bad. I'm all about promoting women in gaming, but this wasn't the right way to go about it. So, I tried to explain these points, and why this female team idea ignored the real competitive advantages of streaming.

I explained that it would fail to build any real relationship between the content creators and the audience—it would involve actors instead of content creators.

It would fail to capitalize on authentic relationships between content creators. Harry was very excited about typecasting these women so that they could appeal to many elements of the market. I believe I still have internal organ damage from the way my body responded when he said, "One of them could even be trans! That's very 'in' right now." But these women wouldn't have been an existing friend group—and that's what you would need to connect with to make a posse work here.

It would fail to—

I got about this far before Harry got bored. He interrupted with a lengthy anecdote about the success of the Spice Girls in the nineties, and committed to the idea that these women wouldn't be *objectified*, so to speak, but it might be a good idea if sometimes they went to the beach in sexy bikinis.

At times like these, when I feel like everyone in the room should be hurling projectile vomit at someone's face together, but I see that nobody else is even gagging yet, I tend to dissociate. I step outside my body and walk around the room and look at everything that is happening and ask myself why it is all so wrong. I finally checked out of the conversation.

One reason I'd been excited to join F2K was that it had been the best org in the world in terms of women in strategy gaming. There's a statement for you to have fun trying to grapple with, almost halfway through this book. The face of the org was a woman who played *Hearthstone*, and several of F2K's other entrenched streamers were women, too. Many of the most successful and respected women in the strategy gaming sphere had done yearlong stints with F2K. The conversation with Harry was not at all what I'd been hoping to hear from a prospective investor.[35]

The most suffocating point in all this was that, while I and a roomful of men were having this conversation, Alliestrasza and Slysssa—two of the most well-known women in *Hearthstone*—were streaming together down the hall. Nicholena had left the previous day. The dynamite women stars of strategy gaming were doing their thing right there with us—I could have opened the door and called them over and they would have heard me—and Harry was sitting in his boardroom talking about spending millions of dollars, but he was talking about setting up interviews for a Middle Eastern woman who would look good in a bikini to appeal to her demographic instead of talking about how to support and empower the women who had fought for years to earn their place in the building with us that weekend. They weren't even invited to the meeting; I was there, and I'm certain the reason I was invited instead of them was that I was a man.

Harry worked quite closely with F2K for several months, and got John and Doug on board with his idea, which never actually went anywhere. Doug eventually approached Nicholena to suggest that she could be the "house mother" and look after the younger[36] women on the team. When I asked her about it, she

---

35 It was, in fact, so bad that I now walk out of movies if I feel like they've been too heavily typecast because I can't help but imagine the executives behind the scenes.

36 Implied: sexier.

told me that her opinion was that guys like Doug and Harry just wanted to build themselves a harem.

Hannah was on a call with Harry exactly once. She got the expected creepy sexist vibes, and managed to pull the right strings so that she never had to talk to him again. He was significantly worse than the guys she was already having to deal with. Every now and then a guy shows up who's so sexist that even the sexist guys you know call him sexist, and Harry was one of them.

Meanwhile, another one of Tyson's staff members had spent some time looking at our business model and financials, decided he couldn't understand how any of us made money despite our best efforts to explain advertising and commission to him, and reported back accordingly. Maybe he was right, in retrospect. It seemed silly at the time, but of course I now know what happened next. He had impressed me when I met him in person.

John eventually claimed to me, through backchannels, that Tyson's team was looking at eight or so different big investments in 2019 without enough cash for any of them, with the intention of raising money from outside investors once they had relationships established. So, they signed a pledge to work with F2K as our exclusive investor, then gave us no money for six months as the contract negotiations stalled and stalled in more and more insulting ways. That could be true—but it seems about equally likely to me that John had been massively overvaluing his company, and the investors he was trying to land worked that out.

Either way, the relationship with Tyson dissolved in late 2019. F2K suddenly found that they had raised no money from anyone at all for half a year, and now their cash cow was riding into the sunset.

BENJI

Six months later, as spring began in 2020, F2K was still struggling. We had never recovered from the Tyson deal falling through. We needed money and we needed money fast. A few other streamers and I had begun taking equity in the company instead of pay. The team had been set up on the legally-favorable island of Guernsey, in the English channel, and was lacking outside investors at this time, so this was fairly easy to set up—or at least that's what I'd been told. Staff were being cut, or cut back, or working almost for free. I don't think any of the streamers taking equity had much expectation of it ever turning into money—we just still liked the team.

I've always been quite confused as to what was so hard about keeping F2K profitable. This was in early 2020, when they still had a contract with Twitch that should have helped them succeed—Twitch was paying them $1,000 a month or so just to have me signed to their team. Twitch was willing to pay F2K for a guarantee that their streamers would make content exclusively on Twitch. Later, in mid-2020, that contract with Twitch ended, and I can understand how F2K's business model could fail after that, but this part was just . . . pretty straight-forward? Take the thousand dollars each month, pay me 50% of it or so, and bring me sponsorships at 15% commission. They had at least fifty streamers signed, easily enough to pay for five staff members, and there wasn't really work for any more than that. There was no physical esports team to send places, no investment money to spend on big things, no physical office space to rent—it was just a bunch of streamers who already made money on their own and wanted a bit more from the market inefficiency that F2K was able to solve.

Part of the problem was that the staff weren't actually all that great at finding good sponsorships for the streamers on the team. There was too much turnover, both in streamers and staff, for people to establish relationships with each other. Many of my sponsorship deals come from people I've known for years, and my brand has been established as trustworthy through an entire career of streaming. New staff who came in didn't have that trust yet, and didn't understand my brand yet either, and increasingly nobody was bothering to do the work to catch up.

Part of it was that the streamers needed wrangling to actually fulfill the sponsorships, which was largely a consequence of the deals' not being particularly good. I suppose that loops back to the first problem.

Part of it was that F2K wasn't a well-known brand, so they didn't have many ways into negotiations and weren't getting emails from potential sponsors. A game developer would rather reach out to me, a respected strategy game streamer, than F2K, a third-tier former esports team.

Part of it was that F2K was constantly looking for some giant home run and, at least in my opinion, neglecting the simple day-to-day stuff that could make them money.

I think the biggest problem was that F2K was paying streamers too much and not asking for enough payment for the advertising they were running on the streamers' channels. I ran a constant, rotating advertising panel on my channel for them for two and a half years, and was told that they never got paid for that by any of the advertisers I was featuring. It was included as part of the "package" when an advertiser signed a contract with the team, instead of being properly recognized as a service worth thousands of dollars by itself.

Fixing their revenue problem didn't seem that hard. Toward the end of 2019, I visited TwitchCon for the first time, and as someone who had no previous experience negotiating large deals, I was able to connect with the CEO of an energy drink company and start a conversation that led to a team-wide energy drink sponsorship for a month in 2020.

This didn't even happen at an exclusive off-site event. I walked up to his booth on the convention floor and talked to him about his product for ten minutes, then asked if he'd like me to bring it up with my team. Hannah's extremely basic and extremely successful strategy for securing sponsorships for me is to respond to emails in my inbox about new games with the suggestion that they could sponsor me to check their game out on stream if they have a budget available for that. In high school, I sold advertising slots in the irrelevant high school newspaper more successfully than F2K seemed to be able to sell advertising slots on streams getting millions of views per year.

One legitimate problem is that once you step outside of game sponsorships—a segment where the developer or publisher of a game will pay for a streamer to show it off on stream for an hour or two—a lot of the products don't match very well with strategy game channels, and the ways sponsors expect them to be marketed don't match at all with the critical thinking inherent to a strategy gaming community.

A basic ask that might be made of me: Here's an energy drink company. Advertise it to your audience and explain how you're excited about it and how it has found better ways of putting unhealthy chemicals in your body than other energy drink companies have.

Okay sure, if you're going to pay me and you need this to not go out of business, I can try.

A second basic ask of me, the next month: Here's a different energy drink company. Without mentioning the previous product, do exactly the same thing for this one.

My viewers aren't goldfish. We have an existing and continuous relationship with each other, and they trust me to have honest opinions. That's the starting premise of why I'd be good at advertising stuff. Pretending to care about a rotating cycle of energy drinks isn't going to work with them, and is going to make me look inauthentic.

My service as an advertiser of products, at least as I sell it personally, is that I am willing to showcase your product to my audience and tell them about it. I don't sell that I'm going to say it's the best product on the market. I don't sell that I'm going to say I personally love it. I don't sell things which aren't true—there's no actual reason for me to do so, and it wouldn't work with my audience. This works fine for game sponsorships—where developers understand that I can't convince my audience that I think a new game is better than the game the community is built around and which I've streamed for five thousand hours—but there is often a significant expectation clash when I'm asked to promote other products. You can sell me promoting a product via product placement, expressing gratitude toward their sponsorship of the stream, and saying things which are true about the product as a neutral endorsement, but a lot of sponsors want more. Frankly, I don't want to give that, and even if I did, they aren't paying enough for it.

I don't know what the answer is to all this friction. Some streamers navigate it just fine, and I am jealous of them. Maybe I spend too much energy thinking critically about consumption to make sense as an advertiser of products, and maybe that's true of a lot of strategy gamers, and the entire space is just doomed for advertising. On the other hand, I generate thousands of click-throughs when I show off a new game, and I don't need to do anything false or excessive; I just tell people what it is and spend a while exploring what's cool about it.

But John never seemed to me like he cared much about any of that. It seemed like a source of frustration for him, rather than something he was passionate about. He seemed to believe that F2K didn't need to solve its small day-to-day failures, because there was always a new big thing that was more important, and he had already found the next one to solve our income shortage. All of our problems were going away, because we'd found the pot of gold at the end of the rainbow. It was—take a second here to pretend I'm doing that bit where someone checks their notes because they don't believe what they're about to say—to sign a year-long exclusive contract with a for-profit charity middleman.

There was a lot to unpack in this.

Charity streams are very successful on Twitch. I'd been running them my entire career because they were fun, great for my community, and great for me. They let me spend time doing something I felt good about: teaching my community about a cause that was important to me, and raising money to support it. I treated them as the zenith of my content—they were the days that I planned for months in advance because I wanted to be showing off the coolest and most unique content I could create. They weren't just about the charity; they were about my community and what we cared about and what we could do together for the world and for each other. Getting your viewers motivated to contribute creatively to your work is one of the cheat codes of streaming, and charity events often succeeded at that for me. I loved everything about them.

The idea of a for-profit charity middleman is that they set up a website to help you connect with a charity, play some alerts on your stream as fundraising goals are hit, and take a cut of the money raised. In the scummiest cases (i.e., the one F2K was signing up for), they'll even pay money to orgs or individual streamers to run these charity events, planning to recoup their costs by siphoning fees or tips off the donations made.

The idea of providing this service isn't completely nonsensical. It's certainly unnecessary—and I usually avoid adding things to my content unless they clearly make it better. But does this make the content better? One useful trick for strategy gamers is to try to come up with reasons you should make the choice that seems less good to you. Sometimes you'll surprise yourself by thinking of a compelling reason.

The main thing it's adding is slot-machine-type attention-grabbing behavior to incite people to donate more toward the goal, but, uh . . . okay, fine; I have trouble justifying it in any way.

I started my career running charity streams where I just linked to the organization's donation page and pledged that I'd also be donating any revenue generated during the stream. The important part wasn't the flashy alerts; it was the moments when I was vulnerable and honest with my audience about something I cared about. But a couple of companies in the space successfully worked out how to make a brand based on other people having those vulnerable moments and filching millions of dollars from them.

There's an argument in utilitarian ethics that the charity middleman is promoting charity work, which causes more good to be done overall, which causes overall improvements to the world. I think this one is bogus too—it's one of those arguments which holds at a surface level if you choose not to think critically about anything at all. Increasing the number of people spending time on charity work, or the number of people donating to charity, doesn't necessarily make the world better. If you're causing those people to do charity work at the cost of their personal comfort, ethics, etc., it can easily make their world worse. If you're convincing people to donate using slot machine tactics, it can easily make the lives of the donators worse. If the charities chosen are similarly profit-focused and similarly prioritize advertising and growth, very little of the money raised may actually end up helping the people who need it. This is just bad territory to be in.

The next sticking point was the "exclusive" part of this arrangement. I was quite confident that F2K could not pledge my charitable nature exclusively to another company. That wasn't part of my contract with them. And it was unclear what that would even mean. Softgiving, the company we were "partnering" with (or more accurately groveling to), had some sort of contractual definition of a charity stream, and it was going to pay us for our streamers to run one of these events every other month, but were they really saying that I couldn't also do charity work online in other ways? What if I wanted to jump into a friend's lobby for a birthday stream where they were raising money for trans rights? Turns out: Yes, the contract was intended to prevent me from doing that. A company claiming to promote charity work wanted to prevent that from happening. Okay. Deep breaths.

I hopped on a call with John and Benji, the "handler" Softgiving had assigned to F2K's contract. Together, John and Benji were going to be in charge of convincing a team of streamers to spend a day every two months asking their communities to give money to a charity which Softgiving selected, using Softgiving's platform—which would ask them to give a tip with their donation. The default tip was an utterly obscene 15%, and a donator would have to click in and manually type a different value if they wanted to, for example, give a $0 tip—just on the off chance that their goal was to fund the charity, not a for-profit company. There's probably some term for the way that this is manipulative, implying that a completely unjustifiable behavior is the expected one through design or whatever.

My entire identity with F2K had revolved around being the charity guy. I'd entered the team by spearheading a huge charity drive, with Hannah organizing everything behind the scenes. A huge amount of my identity as a streamer was based on my charity work. I had a CV which was just for listing my accomplishments in charity fundraising, and I hadn't bothered to make a CV for anything else. A few of the people who worked for the charities I raised money for liked my channel because I accidentally got them hooked on my content when I raised money for them, and some of them kept in touch with me on social media. For the last six months, Hannah and I had been planning a year of climate-related charity work; I was going to raise money for a different cause each month and bring in experts and reading materials to help educate my community about its importance. I went into this call clinging to the hope that Benji would hear about my year of climate charity work and get excited about it, maybe even fling Softgiving's budget behind it, and I could actually get something good from the arrangement.

It's strange to know that a conversation was an immensely pivotal and important moment of your life but not really be able to remember much of it. I think I was too upset and stressed out to be creating many new memories. I remember Benji talked like he was the shit and I was nothing, and that when I tried to explain that I did a lot of charity work on my channel and this contract was going to limit me, he sounded almost bemused. "Ah, so you're all charity all the time," he said in his British accent, like wanting to spend more than six hours every two months on charity made me some kind of unrelatable and monomaniacal magical being. It was not encouraging that someone employed full-time by a company ostensibly devoted to charity work found this aspect of me hard to understand.

I also remember trying to explain that my charity content wasn't packaged in the way the contract outlined. For example, I had people coming into my Discord server for question-and-answer sessions, and a channel for discussing readings about the charity we were raising money for and the issue it tried to grapple with. The "helping-each-other" channel and "lgbtqiaplus-awesomeness" channels in my Discord both became permanent mainstays of the community after their creation had been inspired by charity work for mental health and trans rights, respectively. Did Softgiving expect me to change their names? "lgbtqiaplus-awesomeness-#sponsored-by-softgiving-which-brings-new-and-exciting-ideas-to-the-act-of-raising-money-for-those-in-need" doesn't fit as a channel title. Benji mostly ignored this part. In my experience, when someone's contract clearly asks for things that are impossible to deliver, the norm is for them to either feign ignorance or to actually be ignorant of that fact; with Benji I couldn't tell which of those I was getting.

When all was said and done, I was able to negotiate a few things for myself. For starters, it was okay for me to keep doing a charity stream every month, but Softgiving wasn't going to give F2K any money for the extra ones, despite requiring that I run them through their platform, in the way that they liked, for charities they approved, while exposing my viewers to their tipping infrastructure.

To set up their bimonthly paid charity streams, Softgiving looked at my channel metrics, fed them into "their algorithm,"[37] and decided how much money was reasonable for me to fleece from my community—err, I mean raise for the charity they had picked. That number became my fundraising goal, and four smaller goals were set at 20%, 40%, 60%, and 80% of the target amount. If I reached the total donation goal, F2K would be paid the full amount they were owed for my sacrilege; if not, there were going to be issues.

I also had to set up rewards for my community to "earn" as I hit each fundraising benchmark. Softgiving provided a pre-approved list, and had to approve my final setup before I went

---

37   Please make sarcastic mysterious noises and wave your hands every time you read anything about an algorithm attempting to describe people in any online setting.

live. Here was where Softgiving was at its most unbelievable, with Benji and his colleague Beth doing things like telling people to change their entire stream atmosphere, suggesting that a woman on the team wear a schoolgirl uniform, and telling one of the best *Hearthstone* players in the world that she would raise more money if she pledged to eat dog food. Rereading these chat logs makes my blood curdle.

A particular gripe about a pattern: When someone who is uniquely valued by tens of thousands of people—and with a history of work related to what you're doing—tells you how their community works and what it responds to, don't come back with "We've run thousands of these campaigns now, so we know a good amplifying incentive when we see one. :)" An algorithm is sometimes better than nothing for guiding decisions, but when someone with actual experience working with a particular thing tells you the algorithm is wrong in this instance—especially if they created the thing—you will probably want to listen to them.

Out of all the sexist guys I've worked with in my life, Benji was the most unbelievable. I don't know if he was the most sexist, but he very clearly had absolutely no ability to stop himself from saying the thoughts inside his head out loud. John's sexism was gated and manipulative—he'd deliberately let someone see parts of it, but only as a joke which he could dismiss if they disapproved, or in a situation where he had leverage over them and knew they'd have to play along, or in a context where he was talking about a book or website or other source which he felt made him justified and right. Harry's sexism was presented in an environment where it made sense that he'd feel safe and empowered, surrounded by other men, talking about his lengthy experience in the (also incredibly sexist) Los Angeles entertainment industry. Benji's sexism was neither of these things—it was simply abhorrent and suffocating.

Looking back, I wish I'd been able to communicate with Benji more gracefully than I did. If I'm stretching, I could maybe claim that I barely maintained professionalism with him. Conversations with him felt like he was launching missiles at me non-stop and I wasn't allowed to declare war. Fortunately, Hannah understood exactly how I felt about all this and stepped into the communications as a professional buffer between me and Benji several times. I stopped having to grit my teeth through conversations with him, and started getting helpfully-organized lists outlining my obligations and deadlines from Hannah, instead.

The first charity stream I was scheduled to do under Softgiving's reign fell on my birthday in April 2020, and I spent a decent amount of time leading up to it failing to sleep at night, venting to my partner and friends, and dragging my feet about doing the things Softgiving was asking of me.

Slay the Spire has four different characters, so for this event I set each of my milestone goals as a run with one of the characters where viewers were in charge of making some of the decisions. The reward for hitting the final goal would be a run with all four characters' cards unlocked at once and viewers again in charge. This was a fairly normal—perhaps uninspired—sort of charity event for me. I usually pledged to make some sort of "extra" content related to the games people enjoyed on the channel, but this would have involved a lot more effort from me, and I was feeling drained of energy at the time.

The words on the page look so mundane: A charity middleman, sure, whatever; I see those advertised online all the time. Yet streaming under Softgiving truly upset me and shook my sense of self.

This, I believe, is one of the dangers of language. We talk about experiences in a way which removes us from them—removes the full burden of the emotion that someone actually experiencing them feels. Then, eventually, their emotion is also forgotten—gone like the meaning of the phrase in a game of telephone—and our children are being sold slot machines and our charity work is making a pervy British guy rich and we see that everyone is talking about it but don't have the energy to attach the appropriate emotions to that chatter, and it just becomes . . . normal. How can anyone be expected to find time to care about something like this when another species is extinct, or another town is bombed, but we aren't given the time or energy or context to grieve? When it came out that a streamer I knew had been credibly accused of rape by three people, we were in the middle of the Black Lives Matter movement, and I didn't know if I was meant to try to do something about these specific sexual assaults I was hearing about or stop police murdering Black men, and honestly, I didn't feel like I could do much about either anyway. The people at fault think it's okay, and the people they're surrounded by are trodden on and exhausted.

The online space is full of this. This town was built by selfish, sexist assholes, and we're meant to be grateful to live in it. I don't know how to write this passage and make you feel the rage and hurt that I feel as I write it; all I can do is make it sound like good theater.

My words can even come off as pretentious. How dare I get upset about this when so many people have it so much worse? I certainly don't think I have it worse than others, but I am disgusted and want to scream and want to tell you all everything that I can, and listen to everything that you have to tell me, too, so that we can make it stop.

When I told Hannah that I found this difficult to write about, she offered to help me, and volunteered for the first time that she'd won writing contests in high school and had poetry published. In middle school, she self-published a serial novel under an alias, and the other kids enjoyed passing it around to read. I told her for probably the hundredth time that she was one of the smartest people I'd ever met, and she said, "No, I'm pretty dumb. You can tell from how I wrote it." I want to get so smart that I can find every part of the world that made her, and women like her, say that about themselves, and get so strong that I can roll it all into a ball and throw it into the sun.

***

Hannah and I spent a long time choosing who I was raising money for. I had a few existing relationships with charities I'd been working with for three or more years. My first charity streams were for the DREAM program, which is a peer-to-peer tutoring service which began at Dartmouth University in the United States and has spread to other universities across the country. You take young college students with the world at their fingertips and throw them into tutoring and group learning situations with at-risk youth. It's an awesome charity. The youth get these great young role models, who can expand their horizons as to what's possible. Many of these kids might not have considered going to college otherwise, but nowadays many of the college students who volunteer are former youth participants who have come back to serve in the organization that once served them. At the same time, the college students are forced to look outside of their comfort zone for a second, to see what's happening every day to normal people who didn't grow up in a neighborhood which destined them for the Ivy League—to learn some compassion and patience and humility. Many of the people in this book would have lived completely different lives if they'd spent four years volunteering with a program like DREAM.

Softgiving had an extremely limited selection of charities which they could host events for. This wasn't because they were vetting charities critically and only presenting the ones which were well-run and demonstrating ways to make excellent changes for the world, like I was trying to do. Instead, they were only working with charities that were willing to sign contracts with Softgiving, which I understood to mean agreeing to do things like paying Softgiving for the privilege of being on their website, advertising Softgiving on their own homepage, or pledging to pay a certain amount to Softgiving for metrics that the streamers delivered, such as dollars raised or hours watched. This became a large problem for me, as I didn't have any interest in presenting and selling any of Softgiving's charities to my audience, especially through a charity stream like the ones I'd been running for years and had earned their trust around. After some negotiation, I managed to get Softgiving to let me raise money for any charity I wanted, at least temporarily, as long as I put the charity in touch with them a day or so before the event and let them talk to them about signing a contract to add them to their website.

Now, I didn't trust this. It seemed to me that they were transparently trying to extract money from the charities I had a working relationship with, and that this was a very obvious attempt to get those charities to sign bad deals with them. I shot Mike, the CEO of DREAM, a Facebook message—he was always available to chat about ideas I have for fundraising—and tried to explain the situation without breaking any of the "don't say mean things about us" clauses in my contracts. After I felt like he understood what I was saying, I sent him to talk to Benji. I felt awful, but for a charity that I'd been supporting for ten years, whose CEO I knew personally, I could just barely pull this off.

But in 2020, when Softgiving signed F2K, I was working with lots of new charities which Hannah and I had only been building relationships with for the previous six months. We'd been on calls with tons of awesome people in the nonprofit sector who were eager to make positive change in the world. There was a profound difference between Benji, who would mock my values in passing and then interrupt the conversation to tell me he liked my Spotify playlist, and Anthony, who listened to me patiently on our first call together, acknowledged Hannah in ways which made her feel comfortable working with him, and then spent thirty minutes explaining how his organization, charity: water, was solving problems for charities dedicated to bringing fresh water to people in developing nations. I did not want to send Anthony to have a conversation with Benji. I stopped feeling like I had any agency to build relationships with charities.

I also felt I had no choice but to end some of my existing relationships. In 2019, I was one of the streamers who raised the most money for Trans Lifeline, a support hotline run by trans people *for* trans people, which has a microgrant program to help pay for things like legal name changes. In 2020, when they reached out to me to ask if I'd be one of the figurehead streamers of their next charity drive, I apologized and, in couched language—since, contractually, I couldn't speak honestly about what was going on—tried to explain that I had an obligation to a service which prevented me from being able to raise money for them through the platform they were using. Despite my attempts to distance myself from the decision, the memory of that experience still makes me feel like a pathetic asshole.

People should be judged by their actions, and my choice was to stay with F2K, not only enduring this for myself but also inflicting it on those around me. It is the same mistake I made in my early twenties with relationship abuse, and one of the repeating flaws of my character: an inability to end a toxic relationship with someone I consider to be my team or family. Maybe it goes all the way back to immigrating internationally as a kid; I have spent my entire life since wishing that I could live surrounded by family again.

Back to my first Softgiving charity stream: Another issue was that they had undervalued the amount I was going to raise by a very long way. Hannah tried to explain this to Benji, and he seemed to interpret it as an attack on his ego and his algorithm instead of as her communicating information that both she and I knew about my channel. F2K wasn't going to make any extra if I overshot the goal, and I felt absolutely awful about the entire ordeal, so I planned to basically just dial it in for the day. Show up for the stream and do the bare minimum. I was resigned to whatever might happen.

My community showed up without knowing the surrounding context, and we almost tripled the algorithm's goal for us. I felt . . . mostly bad. Probably the worst birthday of my life. I felt like I had lied to people, more so than at any other time in my streaming career, and I felt like I had hidden behind my personal loss of agency to justify my part in the manipulation, which just made me feel worse. On top of everything else, it was spring of 2020—the beginning of the pandemic. Benji immediately included himself in the accomplishment by using "we" instead of "you" when talking about what Hannah and I were achieving on my channel, and messaged "just like that hey" after having spent the better part of a month insisting I needed to change how I ran my livestream.

In case you missed it, the "just like that" was me building a community for several years, and then me and Hannah planning this event for the past six months: structuring a year of climate charity work; making shortlists of charities to reach out to; and spending hours on calls with different charity representatives, searching for the ones that fit my community best. When Hannah sent him a direct message saying "See! We did it!" he sent a direct message back calling her a "smug bitch." We brought this to John's attention, and he said there was nothing he could do about it. I expressed how I thought that was awful and not okay to Hannah, not yet understanding how normal this type of treatment was for her.

I canceled my year of climate charity work, and when it was time to run another charity stream for Softgiving I figured I'd just suffer my way through it, but I was surprised to find that nobody was asking me to. I asked Hannah what was up and she insisted that I didn't need to do any more of those streams.

This is a part of my story that I'm not going to tell you precisely, because I can't make myself go back and look at the chatlogs, and piece it all together, and understand it, and some of it was deliberately hidden from me. But the gist of it is that Hannah is ferocious and protective, and after my first charity stream for Softgiving, my understanding is that, without consulting me about it because she knew I'd insist on fulfilling my obligation to my team, she told Benji and John that all communication about future charity streams for me had to go through her. Then she told them I was busy. And they kept asking if she'd checked in with me; if I could get on a call with them; when I'd be running my next stream; and she kept telling them I was busy. She told them I was busy for the next six months, every time she got asked, and dared them to tell her she was wrong, and they couldn't make her budge.

I still do charity streams now and then, but increasingly I view them as a way for my community to bring me energy instead of for me to give something extra for a good cause. For my next birthday, in 2021, I set up a stream for charity: water where I pledged to drink nothing except water for one day for every hundred dollars raised. I didn't tell my viewers this—probably I didn't tell it to myself—but deep down I was thinking that a couple of months off soda would help my weight and that I should probably not be drinking alcohol anymore as a general rule. My community raised $36,550, and I couldn't even drink milk or tea for the next year. I was incredibly and genuinely grateful. My then partner, still trying her best to look after me, tried to skirt the rules by infusing jugs of water with cucumber and lemon because she was afraid I'd go insane, but I was blissful about it.

The hardest thing for me now is seeing charity events become more and more common in the space, and no longer personally trusting the ethics of collaborating in them. Charity streams have gone from something I did on my own, with a simple direct link to the charity I was raising money for, to massive corporate affairs, with more than one major company trying to make money off them as a middleman. I used to be excited to receive an invitation to collaborate on a charity event; now I feel scared, unable to tell if it's a good thing to participate in or not, and not having the energy to try to work that out.

At some point, I found myself wondering if I'd just had an unusually bad experience with Softgiving because of Benji, and sent a message to a streaming acquaintance who had worked with Softgiving outside of F2K. I was not expecting a reply— presumably they had signed an NDA, and I had never messaged them before—but I received one anyway. Streamers do look out for each other, a lot of the time. The answer was resoundingly negative. Words like "exhausting," "very little understanding," and "dread" featured in it.

Another friend related being asked by Softgiving to get one of a different team's streamers to do a sexy dance if a fundraising goal was hit. She asked that the request be sent to her in writing, and never brought it up with the streamer in question. When the Softgiving representative she was working with tried to follow up on it, she asked them if they could hear what they were saying.

A charity contact quietly mentioned to me at an event that his boss had warned him that they couldn't work with Softgiving, because Softgiving was failing to publicly disclose the terms of their contracts with streamers in ways which would be legally problematic for the charities they worked with.

Hannah isn't perfect; she can't run the entire world of esports on her own. But if she'd been in charge of Hafu's *World of Warcraft* tournament, I can't imagine that Hafu would have had to deal with a team threatening to sexually assault her being allowed to compete. And if she'd been properly empowered and listened to at F2K, our streamers wouldn't have had to deal with being sexually harassed and belittled by one of our sponsors.

I hope that anyone who started this chapter eager to argue that for-profit charity organizations were an overall good for the world will leave it considering the actual effect that they can have on people who raise money for charities.

CRYPTO

Despite the sexism, failed deals, and horrible contract with Softgiving, one aspect of F2K's business was still flourishing in 2020: anything related to cryptocurrency. I'm not sure it was possible for any business plan involving cryptocurrency to fail anytime between 2011 and 2021. (If you're reading this in the future, I'd be fascinated to know what happens next.)

I had read up on Bitcoin way back in the dark ages when it was around twenty cents per coin, around 2010. A few of the more tech-minded poker players were chatting about it on Two Plus Two, the main publisher of books about poker strategy and the host of the competitive poker community's main discussion forums. The conversation was interesting, but in the way that reading a conversation among people who are convinced they were abducted by aliens is interesting. There were quite a few ludicrously hyperbolic claims, like that its value could easily reach $20. I closed the thread and got back to my life.

A very short time later Bitcoin hit $20, and I decided I should probably read about it some more.

There are elements of cryptocurrency which I like a lot. The general concept of a decentralized way to store information is powerful. In high school, I was tutored in math by a young adult savant whose life goals as of age twenty-five were to make lots of money with black hat coding, defeat China's internet firewall by himself, and find literally any woman who would have sex with him. (It may have been inappropriate for him to share that last part with a teenager in one-to-one tutoring sessions, but if he'd had a clearer understanding of appropriate behavior, he probably wouldn't have had that problem in the first place.) It was easy to think about lots of awesome things that someone like him could achieve with a tool like cryptocurrency if it got big and he grew up.[38]

On the other hand, a system which was meant to operate without reliance on trust wasn't necessarily something I thought I wanted to . . . well, rely on and trust. Trust makes it much easier to function in the world. Hannah is able to provide more for me than an entire esports organization because we trust each other. For a savant battling against Internet censorship, Bitcoin struck me as an interesting tool, but for ordering pizza or investing in assets it was unexciting.

I disliked the currency aspects of Bitcoin, but not really any more than I dislike the currency aspects of any other currency. My experience is that money is useful for facilitating small trades between people—it's nice to be able to pay a few dollars for groceries instead of trying to barter—and creates astonishingly destructive misery in every other way it is used. I'm not trying to say I have a better answer, for what it's worth—often people assume that I'm thinking in a binary when I am critical of our current political or economic systems and that I must support another one instead. I think none of the political or economic systems we invented before the Internet make much sense at all in a world with seven billion people who are connected to each other and are now capable of destroying humanity within my lifetime in at least a handful of different, immediately present ways.

And while the idea of a decentralized currency which could be used extra-nationally to make changes was sort of nice—it

---

38   I feel constantly frustrated at how many savants seem to have chosen one of the central aspects of humanity to use as their dump stat.

might even be the closest thing to a tool capable of instigating massive global change—defining Bitcoin that way felt way too naive for even me to believe in it. It looked, to me, a lot more like its main use was as another tool for a bunch of assholes who cared about wealth and power to get themselves more wealth and power.

Still though, I set up my home PC to mine a bit. At the time, my options when I went to sleep were:

1. Turn the computer off. Save electricity; save the environment.

2. Run Folding@home, a nonprofit computing project which would use my computer processing power to simulate folding proteins and help discover medical advances. Help others.

3. Mine Bitcoin. Make money for myself.

I was okay with picking option three for a little while. It was fun and new, and learning about the experience seemed valuable. In two weeks or so, I mined four Bitcoin at ~$20-30 each, and then got bored and felt like I wasn't achieving anything with real value and uninstalled the mining software. Tracking the price increases was more stressful than seemed worthwhile, so I sold them all at ~$800. It was good for my mental health—I loathed the part of my brain which was constantly wondering how much money they were worth, and the experience contributed heavily to my just hating money and investment in general. There are so many other things my brain needs to think about, and there are only a few years left, one way or another.[39] Wasting a second of my time on the price of Bitcoin seemed inexcusable, and the simple solution was not to have any.

---

39   Of my life, of our world existing like it does, even just of me being in the stage of my life where these are the thoughts which I spend time on. Life is so temporary and capricious; I don't enjoy wasting it.

This was slightly after my active time playing online poker, which had felt much the same. I felt like I could go travel and work on myself, or spend time making teaching content and offering one-on-one poker coaching, or study the game and learn more about it, or—the least appealing option—I could actually play poker, which basically did nothing other than making me money. At times, I was in the mood to play poker and had fun doing it, but it always became harder and harder compared to the other options whenever I had more than enough in my savings account to live on for a couple of years.

I think there are two major beliefs I hold which differentiate me from many strategy gamers. These are my best explanations for why I've tried to build an online community around charity while someone else might join a company trying to capitalize on the expansion of cryptocurrency, or work as a data scientist for a large corporation, or build a pyramid scheme with themselves at the top, or spend their life trying to maximize their own power and manipulate others.

The first belief I hold is pretty simple: I think that we live in a boom-and-bust society, and we are near the end of the largest boom we've ever had, which is about to consequentially be followed by the largest bust we've ever had.

When I have conversations with strategy gamers about this, some agree, but many express incredulity in incredibly logical and intelligent ways. They use the word "Malthusian." A lot of the logic they turn to is flawed, though. They claim that there's no evidence that human societies can go extinct, ignoring that many isolated human populations have gone extinct, and we have studied the ways that it has happened to them. Mostly they've run out of resources they require to survive, or trade routes which they relied on have broken, and then they've all been dead within a generation or two.

The idea of globalization, that we are now a single, interconnected world, exploiting resources everywhere, means that all of us can now enter a bust together, and nobody will be around to bail us out of it. It also means we can now exhaust resources which a society one thousand years ago would have just had brought in by the wind—things like fresh air and rainfall—because the next city over is depleting them all, too. Climate change is a clear existential threat to the entirety of humanity at once, and when we look at previous societies which faced a threat like it without outside help, quite a few of them just kept building bigger and bigger stone heads until they all died. Climate change isn't even the only existential threat right now. We have nuclear weapons pointed at each other while we're trying to navigate these threats.

In such a world, I simply don't think it's a great idea to spend one's life being selfish. I think if we all focus on ourselves our entire species will likely be extinct quite soon.

The second belief goes like this: Say you see someone express some ludicrous or stupid or evil belief on the Internet. They think Elvis was an alien, or Trump won the election in 2020, or they hate a certain type of people, or whatever. There are very different conclusions you could take away from this.

Here's a common one: Haha! I am a rational and sensible human being, and this other human being is not. Humans like me are better than humans like that one. Once again I have found justification that my own beliefs are right by observing how wrong the beliefs of people who aren't like me often are.

And a much less common one: Uh oh. I am a human being, and so is that person. This is further evidence that we can have our brains go haywire and believe incorrect and hurtful things. Once again I've found evidence that my own beliefs are likely to be wrong, that I'm stuck in a world where biased evidence can lead me to the wrong conclusions over and over again.

I think the second one. The first is, in my opinion, an utterly ridiculous thing to believe. Occasionally there is also evidence of humans doing great things, and I'm a human like them, too, so I don't believe I'm entirely flawed. But that's a small shelter in a storm of evidence that I'm probably a gigantic idiot like so many others. The world is simply too complicated for us to understand it all, so we settle for simple behaviors which we can't actually justify, hoping that they'll be good enough.

The truth, in my opinion, is that almost all of our behaviors are harmful and wrong, but we just don't really care. We humans know what we want to do and, when the mind of a strategy gamer goes haywire (which is usual and normal; that's what human minds often do), they use their arguments and ideas to justify doing it. It's a defense mechanism against the intimidating amount of grief and pain waiting for you if you reach the other conclusion—that almost all of your behaviors are likely to be hurtful and baseless and wrong. I'm a professional strategy gamer, and one of the most respected *Slay the Spire* players on the planet, and I still make extremely simple mistakes in *Slay the Spire* all the time. Do you really think it's likely that I'm getting all the other stuff in my life right?

It can be very unsettling to watch the cogs turn in someone's brain to justify continuing doing something that they know is wrong but don't want to change. A lot of people I know were smart kids who grew up hearing non sequitur arguments from parents and peers about meat consumption, like, "When I go to the grocery store, the animal has already been killed, so if I don't buy the meat and eat it, it would just be going to waste." These are nonsensical and empty arguments which crumble under examination but which absolve us of personal responsibility if they are never questioned.

But then the kids grow up, and they really like eating meat—a dietary craving that's more decided by things in your body like your stomach bacteria than by any logical, conscious thoughts—and so they find their own argument which they will never question in order to absolve themselves of personal responsibility, too. "It would just be going to waste" morphs slightly into "The corporation that killed this animal is too large for my individual actions to affect anything. I might as well just buy the meat—the real way to make change is through voting and protest." Note of course that these people usually aren't racing out the door to vote or protest, either.

"What about corporations?" is just the most common argument for personal absolution, a lukewarm reskin of "It's already been made anyway." When I talk to some of the most impressive strategy gamers I know, people who were celebrity role models for me ten years ago and whom I'm lucky enough to be able to get on the phone with today, they express much more complex ideas. They suggest we make a friendly wager on whether or not the climate predictions of the entire scientific community end up being wrong, winking at me that they have personal reason to believe that they will be. Or they say things like, "A bit of hedonism toward the Earth is necessary for us to function"—not claiming they aren't doing something bad as much as pointing out that there's no way to avoid doing bad things, which I think is absolutely true. I also think we should probably be spending at least an hour a week grieving over it and trying our hardest to change it.

There seems to be a huge movement around denying that individual action has any meaningful effect on climate anyway, which is incredibly difficult to grapple with. It is wrong—a recent study suggests an average American will kill one-third of a person with their personal emissions over their lifetime[40]—and this

---

40 Almost any functional ethical system would mandate that you do simple things within your power to reduce the likelihood of killing people. That there are other bad actions does not excuse your living

study doesn't consider runaway scenarios or even any causes of death other than heat—but it is compelling and easily resonates with people. A viral argument right now is that our focus on individual action is because of a marketing campaign by British Petroleum (maybe some of it is, but mine certainly isn't) and that individual actions only serve to distract from lobbying lawmakers for collective action. Hank Green, science communicator and author, speaks more succinctly about this tension than I could, explaining that he liked that argument when he heard it, but when he looked up research about it, he found that collective action is more likely to happen if individuals are acting like there is an emergency than if they're acting like there's nothing they can do about it. He points out that it's often possible to find correct evidence on the Internet, but laments that it's even easier to find incorrect evidence which is emotionally appealing.

My suggestion? Just admit that you're wrong and don't know everything. When I play a complex strategy game, I never believe that I have solved something to a point where there is no way I could possibly improve it. But when strategy gamers navigate life, they like to pretend that they've found the perfect solutions to things all the time.

And so I recognize that I'm imperfect. My command of logic is at the whims of the physical needs and desires of my body. I *could* live in a way that was much lower-impact, but I'm comfortable and stuck where I am. It's an empowering thing to

---

your life in ways which are unnecessary and which kill people. Nobody is asking you to go live in the woods. It would just be nice if you'd make simple changes like turning your lights off at night, eating less meat, and flying less, if those are changes which you are empowered to make. The more empowered you are as an individual, the more ethical responsibility you carry for the consequences of your actions, and most people I know are among the most empowered humans who have ever lived in the history of our species.

admit. I'm *human*. All of a sudden, I don't have to be right all the time anymore. All of a sudden, I can start actually logically analyzing my actions and finding things to change without hating myself. I can admit past mistakes. My capacity for analysis and strategy stops being a defense mechanism and starts helping me be a better person.

Do that, and then spend some time learning how to change behaviors, because it isn't just about saying you're going to do something different. Read books about habit forming, or hire a productivity coach to help you build new ones. When you have extra time and energy, spend it on restructuring your physical life so that it's easier to make good choices and harder to make bad ones. Environmental changes are a big deal—a lot of the time it's useful to think of yourself as a plant with a brain in it, and make sure that you're getting water and sun and other basic chemical requirements for healthy existence. Just slowly make small improvements, based in kindness and love, using whatever energy you can find for yourself to make them with. If everyone did that, all the time, humanity would be unstoppable.

***

If you're completely out of the loop, Bitcoins are worth around $20,000 each as of the writing of this draft, and they and other cryptocurrencies are all the rage in tech circles, although their useful applications in the world as something other than speculative investment are a little unclear. They're still completely unstable. In fact, when I first wrote this chapter in 2021, they were worth around $50,000.

When I get massive influxes of donations on my channel, I sometimes check the price of cryptocurrency to see if someone is sharing the wealth from their net worth suddenly doubling. The production of greenhouse gases to enable Bitcoin's use currently compares to that of a medium-sized country, and, if you jump on a search engine and look for articles, you can find a tremendous number of miserably flawed but emotionally appealing attempts at explaining why that isn't a problem.

A particularly successful crypto sponsor of F2K was Rally, a site that allows creators to make their own cryptocurrencies which are part of the Ethereum blockchain. I knew relatively small streamers who mentioned having a million dollars in their personal coin, grown from a tiny initial investment. Now, that didn't actually mean they had a million dollars. It was unrealistic to think that they could sell all their crypto at its current price. But they were doing pretty well with it.

I had a passing familiarity with cryptocurrency and was sort of curious what Rally was all about, so I pulled some strings and got a call with Oliver, an employee of the company, in its early stages. He was in a spacious meeting room in the Bay Area. I videoconferenced in on some big TV screen while he walked around the physical space of the room entirely alone, screen sharing the bare-bones presentation he had made to explain what was going on.

The basic idea was that creators had their own currency which they could use for tournaments, giveaways, etc., and it was a subcoin of Ethereum, one of the main cryptocurrencies. Okay. I asked a few more questions about why this was so exciting, and he seemed perturbed—I got the sense that usually when people received this presentation, their eyes glazed over and they reached for their wallets as soon as they heard "blockchain." I couldn't tell if he thought I was too dumb to understand what cryptocurrency was or too dumb to understand that it was obviously a magical being which would make us all rich.[41] He went deeper and deeper

---

41   It is quite unsurprising and logical for people who have made millions of dollars off cryptocurrency without even having to do anything to think that cryptocurrency is a magic beanstalk. This belief, while con-

into the presentation, ending up on slides which he said he hadn't quite finished yet, and I was still uninspired.

The biggest point of confusion for me was how exactly Rally planned to make money. They were willing to back the first few creator coins they set up, meaning that they'd have some portion of them, but what exactly were they doing to get money other than that? Were they siphoning parts of the giveaways? What was happening here?

Rally was, of course, in phase two of the money chain in tech—the part where they have lots of money, and their business model doesn't need to make any sense. If I had been more cutthroat and excitable, maybe I would have jumped on that and set up my own creator coin, planning to ditch it in a year or so, but my takeaway was that I didn't trust them, and I remembered it having been stressful to keep track of the ups and downs of crypto the last time I'd been invested in it. Crypto had had almost another full decade to mature since then, and I still didn't love how it looked. The ultimate turnoffs for me were that the climate was in major trouble and crypto was making it worse, and that I didn't like wealth disparity and the only thing crypto had done so far was exacerbate it. It wasn't something I was eager to support. So I passed.

It turned out that, at that time in the history of the world, having an investment of any sort in cryptocurrency was a successful business model by itself, and Oliver and his company's wealth skyrocketed. Later, I would come to know a lot more about him, after he joined F2K as its co-CEO, but for now let's leave him, his team, and anyone who invested with them, flying toward the moon on their crypto rocket.

---

sistent with their experience, is unfortunately inconsistent with simple logical observations about the world.

THE MEADOW

The life of a streamer isn't all bad! Some of it's really, really good.

There's a happy medium in between the streamers who share your audience and the people who know nothing about you, where rich soil is waiting to blossom into easy and rewarding friendships. I think about compatibility like this: For each pair of people, imagine a board of ten switches. If someone is just like me, all ten switches on our board are turned on. I'm not exactly sure what each switch refers to, but the closer we are to five, the easier it is to become real friends with someone. Even just getting down to eight or so makes it manageable—streaming a different game from them at a different time of day, maybe. But a relationship based in that often feels monosyllabic. You can relate on a lot of things, which is fun at first, but then over time you realize that you relate on *too* many things. Neither of you has anything interesting to add. So, start shifting more variables. Maybe the person doesn't actually stream games—they make games, or they write books about them. The community they build isn't on Twitch; instead they run a communal housing project. These conversations get very interesting and impossibly complicated very fast. When I meet someone like this and we share mutual affection, I usually feel like we are both trying to hold ourselves back to avoid coming off as overeager.

In the beginning of 2020, F2K was floundering through the last reserves of its cash. There were murmurs about some respiratory illness in China, which soon became an exhausting challenge to navigate as an entertainer, and Hannah and I were slogging onward with our year-long climate charity project. Softgiving was little more than a rumor at F2K at this point. The first month went almost entirely to plan, which was wonderful. An old poker friend came on the channel to talk about individual productivity with us, and we spent some time learning how to change our behaviors in the face of new challenges. It was a good month. Month two was about motivation, and it was transcendent.

Char is a writer who has worked on a few big videogame projects—RPGs like *Divinity: Original Sin* and *Baldur's Gate*. She got into *Slay the Spire* in a big way in 2019 and she, her partner, and her boss at the indie studio where she works still play the daily challenge every day. She liked my content and reached out on Twitter.

It's relatively easy to keep up with most messages you receive as a one-hundred-thousand-follower entertainer. That sounds like a lot of people, but most of them just don't send you messages very often. It takes five to ten minutes a day to read all my incoming YouTube comments, Twitter messages, and private emails. I had an interesting moment of connection with a friend who had just published a book featured on *Good Morning America*, where each of us expressed some surprise and appreciation for the other being able to make time for us—and then we both realized that neither of us was actually very busy. Socially drained and working hard, sure, but plenty of free time still exists if you decide that you want it and set boundaries accordingly.

So, when I see a message from a new person, I'll often take a moment to hover over their name to see a little bit about them. I love this function of Twitter, compared to the complete facelessness of messages from Twitch users. I saw that Char was a writer. That was cool. I loved talking to writers. I even wished I was a writer myself sometimes. I clicked through to her profile and saw that she had her own website, and that her pinned tweet was about her giving a workshop at CERN, and I was already blown away. I clicked through to her website and started playing the first talk she had linked. In her entrancing Irish accent, she begins the hour-long lecture by leading breathing exercises and seated yoga stretches for the audience.

I have started that lecture three times and never made it past five minutes. I have absolutely no idea what she says in it. Every time, her calmness and timbre take me to a place of peace which is part of my world but which I only ever visit when forced to on vacation. I suddenly don't want to be at my desk anymore, and I stand up and begin cleaning my apartment, or go outside for a walk.

I reached back to her, and we eventually set up a chat, and I got to meet her partner, Martin, who was just as interesting. He was teaching game design at a university and working on an AI-generated card game. And I introduced my then partner, Caitlin, and she got along with both of them. And I was suddenly floating in an ocean of joy.

We became occasional guest characters in each other's lives. Char recommended a few other people I could follow, and I loved them all. I played games that her indie studio released on my stream. She started teaching online weekly yoga courses, and Caitlin and I signed up and made an effort to get flexible and find the bliss that she was full of for ourselves. I designed my own character for *Slay the Spire* and got her help writing voice lines and suggesting lore. I recommended a game to her because it made me think of her energy, and she smiled and told me that she knew the writer and had privately consulted on the ending. Martin and I chatted about card game design, which went a little over Char's and Caitlin's heads, and they chatted about knitting, which went way over ours. I sent her the first draft of this book, and she devoured it. She told me it was like walking through a beautiful meadow, and drew attention to moments where

I'd been too crass or dismissive, describing them as thorns she snagged on along the way.[42] I thought, yes, I know that meadow, I visit it every time we talk.

In January 2020, I had explained the mechanics of how someone could change their behavior to respond to the challenges presented by climate change. In February, I wanted to motivate *why* someone should. So I asked Char to join me on stream alongside Jason, the figurehead of Rise Above The Disorder, a mental health charity which had grown out of a *World of Warcraft* guild and his own struggle against depression, and we chatted for an hour and a half about purpose and motivation. Char led a couple of meditations, to center us as we began our conversation, and to send us back to the world as it ended. She raved on Twitter afterwards about how this was a standout moment in her life in gaming. After years of finding cruelty and misery in every community she looked at, she was amazed to have led meditations on Twitch and to have had a gaming audience participate and enjoy and applaud.

Yeah. Sometimes it's good in ways that words can only hint at.

And then of course Softgiving rolled in and destroyed the entire rest of the year. Streaming feels, at times, like an endless battle to surround yourself with the people who are good and kind and wonderful, trying as hard as you can to pick them out amongst the tide of people who have arrived where they are because they are manipulative and cruel and selfish. When you succeed, you make beautiful things, but when you fail …

I have blackout film on the windows of my office so that I can control the light in the room, and as I write, I have the window

---

42   As I mentioned in Support, I tend to dissociate when dealing with extremely stressful situations, and that was unfortunately a some-what common occurrence as I wrote this book. Each subsequent draft brought a little more emotion and presence to what I'd written, but at some point I had to say "this will do!" and finally publish it.

open just a sliver to let in a fresh breeze without too much of the morning cold. Looking at the heartless, deep flatness of the blackout contrasted next to the vibrant waving trees outside, I think, "Huh, those two right next to each other, that's streaming." And I wonder how far I can get the window open.

***

In the fall of 2020, F2K went to Indy's Techstars Sports Accelerator, a few whirlwind weeks in which selected businesses joined workshops, solicited wisdom, and practiced pitches with a bunch of advisors and potential investors. It was held remotely in 2020 because of the coronavirus, but John and a couple of other staff disappeared off into conference calls for an unreasonable number of hours.

Eventually, I got the call-up to speak on a couple of panels with potential investors who were interested in hearing about the company. The second half of 2020 wasn't particularly kind to me; I managed to uncharacteristically sleep through the beginning of the first panel, arriving eight minutes late, but I think I played it off fairly gracefully. The celebrity streamer, showing up after the dull parts of the conference call in the same way he might glide into a party at the exact right moment— entirely intentional, entirely under control, looking a little like he just rolled out of bed, but in a way that probably took him three hours to style to perfection.

As usual, I was introduced as "the talent," the only guy on the call who actually streamed, along with a bunch of guys in a variety of occupations and one woman—Nancy—who I immediately assumed was the sharpest and most competent person in the group. There was just no chance that a woman who had made it onto this call wasn't a superlative human being. As it turned out, she'd come up through Nike and had been heavily responsible for the marketing success of both the WNBA and the US women's national soccer team.

These calls are never very interesting to me. Guys who don't actually have experience streaming talk about what streaming is and also mention the size of its market cap, which inevitably leads to five-minute diversions as we try to define which market we're talking about: Did we mean streaming on Twitch, or esports tournaments, or YouTube content, or ... what exactly did we start talking about this for anyway? It always feels like three languages are being spoken: There are the investors, who understand money, and the streamers, who understand streaming, and the staff—in this case employees of F2K—who had opinions about what F2K was doing or could be doing, and a lot of the conversation might be spent on miscommunications between these languages.

I began to lose interest as I spent five minutes listening to someone make the point that the time to ask whether esports were real sports was five years ago. It was unclear how esports related to F2K at all—we hadn't had a team in years and predominantly had a roster of recreational strategy game players.

I did my best to explain what streaming was to the potential investors and also a few of the F2K-aligned people who seemed like they didn't know yet. It's me entertaining a bunch of people with a live show online; they have a chat room; my revenue comes from payments they make (repeating subscriptions or one-time donations), advertising, sponsorships, and contracts like the one I had with F2K. The last time I fully did my accounting, I managed to find thirteen revenue streams, including one I hadn't collected my payments from in the last eighteen months, so it gets a little complex, but the general idea is simple enough. I talked about the community-building elements and compared it to watching a professional athlete or comedian perform, but also being able to participate in a conversation with them at the same time. We talked about alerts and other attention economy frills, such as buttons which ask a viewer to press them to share a notification on the main show which says, "Hey, a viewer by the name of [their name here] has subscribed for [number of] months in a row," and then the streamer says, "Hey, [their name], thanks for the [number of] months subbed," and maybe does something goofy and entertaining to express their gratitude. The investors asked some sensible questions, like how my revenue breaks down proportionately into those different categories. I shared some things which I thought were important for them to understand about my motivations: I was only contracted to F2K, and I was more interested in my personal enjoyment and health than in making them money.

At the end of the call, Nancy brought up that she was the only person present with she/her pronouns, sort of as a closing remark, and I wished that she had brought it up earlier because (as you may have noticed) I think there's an awful lot to say and recognize about the treatment and placement of women in this space. Later, I ended up getting John to connect us via email, and I set up a call with her and a few of the women I knew in the space to share their perspectives. Nancy brought a couple of other superstars to the call too. It was pretty cool. She told Nicholena that she should trademark the phrase "Zen yourself," after Nicholena shared about her struggle and eventual success at stopping her audience from seeing her frustration when she lost games.

That meeting I would sit in for an hour every morning for the rest of my life.

***

Finding female voices in this space can be difficult. A paper examining the difference between the chat messages sent to male and female streamers found that, while streams with lower viewership sometimes had a lot of similarities between sexes, the most popular female streamers had two main options to choose between in order to run a massive channel. Some fully embraced the teenage-male-dominated space by leaning into their sexuality, and their channels were full of messages about boobs and other examples of people being horny in public. I find these women impressive and incredible, harnessing the indiscretions of their viewers' ids to earn themselves money and fame. While their importance and success might suggest dark things about the health of our society's sexual relationships, it is undeniable that they are important and successful, and it is not their fault that people find them sexy. Many are able to be extremely frank and authentic with their audience, and have boundaries established around the limits of their comfort which allow them to provide powerful entertainment. There are plenty of negative things I could mention, too, but they get said all the time, almost always unproductively, and I'm tired of them. It's very hard to claim that any of them are these women's faults.

The other option seems to be extremely strict moderation and boundary setting. In these channels, the paper found that the names of moderators ended up being some of the most frequently used words. In a world where a bunch of (predominantly) guys are drooling over a woman's appearance, a successful strategy is to deny attention to that desire and redirect the attention into a focus on what they are doing and how they are otherwise impressive. For example, Sasha Grey, well-known for her career in pornography, now runs a moderately successful channel on Twitch which is focused almost entirely on gaming and is almost entirely non-sexualized.[43]

---

43 Her decision to avoid sexualizing herself doesn't mean that others won't choose to, though. I found myself grimacing as I watched a clip of one of the world's most popular male streamers attempting to banter with her on a quiz show he was hosting, describing her decision

Imane Anys, known online as Pokimane, has an astonishingly beautiful presence and brand, but masterfully teases the edges of sexuality to keep viewers interested and refocus them on her personality and charisma, managing to take the absolute best elements of both of these archetypical audience appeals and forge them into a positive and authentic community. When the sexuality-based streamers found a loophole in Twitch's rules which allowed them to wear bikinis in situationally appropriate settings and abused it by installing hot tubs in the studios and filling them ankle-deep with water,[44] Imane teased that she was going to convince all of her friends at OfflineTV to do a hot tub stream with her for her birthday, and then showed up to it wearing a T-shirt with a bikini top printed on it. When another woman was banned for a few days after a wardrobe malfunction (often a result of bad wardrobe decisions paired with alcohol) had showed a lot more than was allowed and appropriate for a website showing advertising to children, Imane said that she was shocked by it, but she also grinned at the camera and mentioned that, when she saw how well the clip was performing metrics-wise, it had gotten her businesswoman brain churning.

I like women—I like humans, and that affection doesn't have much to do with their gender—and I have been frustrated for my entire life that it has been difficult to share experiences with them in strategy gaming. Even women who I'm dating and living with—and who are interested in the games I play—have bounced

---

to go with a different answer from her competitors as "Sasha Grey vs. three guys" and saying that that "sounded familiar" to him. Comments on the clip lauded him and called him a hilarious Chad.

44　This actually happened and isn't even all that high on the list of most absurd things which have happened on Twitch. More recent lowlights have included crypto casinos spending millions of dollars on advertising to children and constant raids targeted at marginalized streamers consisting of thousands of chatbots spamming hate messages.

off them because of the toxicity with which they are treated when we play these games with others. Female and nonbinary friends are less likely to make the initial effort, and even less likely to stick around after they see what happens. The situation is slowly getting better, with many of these women of Twitch leading the way, but the work is still far from complete.

In trying to lend my modest weight to this, I've reached out to many women, hoping to set up collaborations and showcase them on my channel. It has been hard. A lot of the time, there is no clear way to contact them at all—while I could shoot a direct message to a man and get a response back in an hour, sending the same message to a woman who streams will often yield an automated response: "Message was not delivered due to privacy settings." If I do manage to start a conversation with them, it often feels labored, like the person I'm talking to has had hundreds of guys try to initiate contact with her just because they want her attention and want her to love them—which makes sense, because they all *have* experienced this.

Many streamers are very social people, but we all put that social energy into our channels, and when we're offline we still have incoming emails and messages and other requests to respond to, so I've found that it's actually quite unusual for streamers to make extra time to reach out to each other. I treasure the times that they do. Male streamers will reach out to me from time to time for a variety of reasons, and I get lots of messages from viewers who are men as well, but in all of the time I've spent streaming, only an incredibly small number of women have reached out.

This culture of strategy gaming isn't just bad for women; it's bad for men, too! We game in a space where half of the potential players are immediately alienated. Twice as many people could be setting new world records, crafting new games, or setting up fun tournaments, if we'd let them in and treat them with respect.

THANKSGIVING

ere in the States, as 2020 ground onward, we made our own rules for ourselves in the pandemic. Government response was all over the place. It is very hard to make choices when loss of human life is involved. As a child, I'd thought my mother was lying to me when she told me you couldn't put a dollar value on a human life, and now, as an adult convinced that she had told me truthfully that there was none, I wonder if that's actually how people are making decisions about the way our country is run. I saw people politicizing death and, later in 2021, refusing miraculous vaccines which could save them and others, and wondered how the world could possibly be so cruel.

I'd simultaneously thought that the pandemic would be much harder and also that far fewer people would die. I'd thought infrastructure would shut down and I wouldn't be able to order food from my favorite restaurants, for example. It turned out that, instead, we just kept the restaurants open, and the workers got sick and took the disease home to kill their elderly relatives. I'd thought I'd be paying extra taxes to cover huge relief bills; instead we just let people lose their jobs and get evicted. What relief the government did send seemed to go mostly toward large businesses, not my neighbors. Over one million Americans have died from the coronavirus—another number which became too big for me to understand.

I mostly chose to maximize safety. I stayed inside, at times realizing it had been two or more weeks since I'd opened the front door to take so much as a walk. I am still the stupid guy who thought he could endure two years of relationship abuse for some nebulous benefit to an abuser who openly despised him, and I diligently fell back into that pattern with society as my new partner and coronavirus as the new cancer. I was no longer trying to help only one person's mother—now I was trying to protect them all.

My then partner and I went out for groceries together the first couple of times. She'd made some homemade masks out of loose fabric and elastic. They didn't fit our faces very well and irritated my skin, but it felt good to have something. After that, advisories suggested that people shouldn't be in groups when grocery shopping in order to reduce the number of people in the stores, so she started going alone.

We wiped perishables down before putting them in the fridge, and left everything else out on the floor for three days before we touched it. We washed our hands a lot, and learned song segments which were twenty seconds long to time ourselves.

Her employer, an after-school program, jumped through a variety of despicable hoops to try to stay open as long as it could, and again it was never clear whether the person in charge was actually ignorant or feigning ignorance. Observation: It doesn't matter much—they're doing something awful either way.

We set up a coronavirus test for her when I heard a strange ping on my computer, and eventually worked out that it was an old friend reaching out on a messaging service I'd forgotten I had to say he had a hookup. A woman we didn't know met her outside Home Depot in hazmat gear and shoved something up her nose in the parking lot. A couple of weeks later, we finally heard that the test was negative.

She eventually got an email that basically told her, "If you're uncomfortable, you can opt out of work (but the people who opt in are the only ones we'll be paying)." She quit. My parents employed her to work for their online business after she started to get stir-crazy from a couple of months sitting on the couch.

Later, while this was all still going on, she was accepted to a grad school program in counseling and even did very well in the classes, despite having had bad prior experiences with online learning and desperately needing to be in physical spaces with other people. I loved her and was proud of her. After a few months, she risked a camping trip with her parents, just for a few days. Even in such a short time, I felt parts of me falling to pieces because she was gone.

Meanwhile, I just . . . kept working. I mostly didn't even take a day off. The world was collapsing around me, but when was it not?

I'm happy, most of the time. Sometimes I get into funks, but most of the time . . . yeah, "happy."

My emotions tend not to connect properly to what is happening around me. That's been a thing since the relationship abuse, I think. I don't get super happy and animated at parties or around other people I like—I'm just sort of there with them. I cry a healthy amount, but it's at completely random times. Sometimes I'll notice I'm wound up and think, "Oh, I haven't had a good cry in a while," and I can basically schedule one for myself. Take the night off to watch bad rom-coms, or an afternoon for a hike somewhere secluded, and if I need a cry, it'll be coming out, guaranteed. But when an actually sad thing is happening, I close off and deaden my emotions. So, I kept working, and I was— well, maybe not happy. Functional, though.

The norm for me is to put all of my emotional energy into streaming. My emotional energy runs out significantly before I need to sleep, most days. So, the stream gets six to eight hours of me with my emotional energy intact, and then the rest of the world gets what's left. Sometimes I have to stream when I'm not feeling great—a sponsored stream that's scheduled for a certain day, for example—and viewers will catch on that I seem pretty dead and not fun, and some of them will express concern and ask if something's wrong or complain that I'm not at my best. That's what I'm like for almost everyone else in my life almost 100% of the time that they get to spend with me. I give streaming everything.

I noticed a few changes during the pandemic. I went from hating Twitter and thinking it was a vacuous wasteland—prying at my brain and manipulating me into reinvesting my creativity into its ecosystem while selling my data to advertisers—to still thinking that, but now I was also using it a lot more and feeling like it was my main method of social interaction. I went from walking outside once or twice a day to pacing back and forth in my apartment. A variety of plans, routines, and habits that I had spent years building for myself because they enabled me to function properly stopped being practicable, and I didn't have any time or energy to examine what was going on and adjust them, so I just kept working and kept functioning as well as I could. I gained ten pounds and then another ten pounds. My fancy, two-thousand-dollar customized bed stopped feeling as comfortable as it had when I'd bought it just two years ago, so I lay awake, wondering if the company had overpromised and I should complain, or if I'd just gotten too fat for it. My troubled sleep took me to faraway places and different times, landing me in bizarre stress dreams where I forgot to bring my mask to the grocery store and was forced to wear a communal one, damp with other people's sweat, or where I grew old and became politically conservative. I often woke up disoriented, confused about where I was and what was happening.

I used to hate speaking about politics on stream, but the pandemic changed that. The political conversation was no longer complex—there was a clear correct action as presented by scientists and medical professionals, and it was only opposed by a bunch of greedy and selfish humans who were motivated by personal gain or who genuinely didn't understand the germ theory of disease and didn't realize they needed to shut up. And at the same time, I used to speak about interesting events in my own life, or chat with viewers about theirs, and none of us had much to say anymore, so I needed something to replace it with.

Incredibly few people expressed compassion or gratitude for my entertaining them through this awful time. On my good days, I was able to maintain the illusion that it was easy, and on my bad days, they started complaining that I wasn't doing it very well. If I tried to express how hurtful it was that I was surrounded by thousands of people all day who barely expressed any empathy toward me as a human being, I was mostly told that my job was easy and I was killing the vibe. A few people were genuinely kind, and I sheltered beneath their words like they were a doorframe in an earthquake.

Come Thanksgiving, I had been inside for more than half a year, reaching into the deepest crevices of my brain to somehow convince thousands of people that I was still entertaining. I had lost all belief that I was an interesting person, so I tried to be a comfortable one. I had lost belief that the world was kind, but maybe I could be that for people. I have never felt attractive and certainly didn't then, and also shaving felt like a bit too much work at the time, so my webcam stayed off more and more often. My glasses prescription was getting outdated, and the lighting on my face for the camera was starting to seriously strain my eyes, and I couldn't get an optometrist appointment, so that sort of had to happen anyway.

After my first Softgiving stream in April 2020, I had largely stopped making new memories, and this continued all the way through to the Spring of 2021. I'm not sure how much of it was that my brain wasn't functioning anymore and how much of it was that there just wasn't anything worth remembering. Either way, I can't remember much of what happened. I drank a lot, played *Among Us* with friends, and survived. I wish I could tell you what snapped me out of it, but I don't remember that, either. When I started feeling human again, I observed that I weighed twenty pounds more than before and hadn't cashed multiple paychecks.

On Thanksgiving morning, 2020, I had been up all night. It was hard, during this time, to tell how long I was going to need before sleeping after a stream. It took anywhere from five minutes to five hours to re-center myself energetically, and after that, I needed anywhere from five minutes to five hours of "me time" to do things that I wanted to do on my own. Sometimes I wanted to spend time with my partner; sometimes I didn't. Maybe we'd have an argument, and it'd throw everything off for me some more. None of these variables related very sensibly or predictably to anything else; it felt like they were just sort of happening to me.

Relationship arguments with a streamer might be hilarious to an outside observer. They are grindy and miserable to actually participate in, but on our good days, my partner and I could see the humor in our miscommunications when she did things which would be completely normal to any other human being but which elicited perverse stress responses from someone used to thousands of faceless viewers criticizing and demanding and reacting to the things that he did. Simple questions she asked me, like, "Are you planning to do [x] tonight?" hit weird, wound-up parts of my psyche and made me think of hundreds of different people, slowly melting away my will with never-ending requests for me to do exactly what they wanted. It was hard to be present for a relationship while I was losing track of who I was in a sea of other peoples' voices.

I used to feel like I was getting the hang of understanding how my body and brain worked, but 2020 changed all that. So sometimes I was up all night.

During this period, everything was also especially weird with F2K. Hannah was back with the team, and she was feeling like she really needed her paycheck from them, but new staff were coming in on the back of a big investment round after Techstars, including Oliver from Rally as a new co-CEO, and we didn't know what was going on. When I'd taken equity instead of pay at the end of 2019, it was with the belief that a corporate investment in F2K would mean me cashing out and leaving—I hadn't wanted to be part of a transitional corporate team structure—but we were somehow heading straight to corporate without the intermediary step where I would've gotten a chance to cash out. And so it was Thanksgiving morning, and I was still up, and Hannah had just woken up.

Hannah and I have a way of breaking each other down into cleansing tears. We understand so much about each other's lives, and respect each other deeply. She'll tell me something like, "You always say things that make me tear up for far better reasons than what used to make me cry," and then I'll think about that and tear up, too, at the things she's leaving unsaid.

I used to think that the coolest thing you could do if someone told you that they loved you was say, "I know," like Han Solo in *Star Wars*, but when I told Hannah I loved her for the first time, she showed me I was wrong by not even acknowledging what I'd said. She just responded to the other thing I'd said in the sentence because it was more important. A few weeks later she told me that she loved me, and I understood fully: there wasn't anything to respond to—we both already knew. And there were no boundaries to negotiate or questions about whether this was meant romantically or anything else. We just both understood what we meant, and that was that. Our friendship started as a mutually respectful business relationship, but by that Thanksgiving . . . well, we'd already been through a lot of shit together, and there was more to come.

I don't remember who called whom or why. We probably needed to chat about something mundane. She was chopping food, getting started on preparing Thanksgiving dinner for her parents and friends, and I was sitting with my window open, listening to the birds wake up, a couple of time zones west from her. I think we were talking about new graphics we could commission for the channel. I suggested a little drawing of me playing guitar, and she said, "I didn't know you played guitar!" and I said, "oh yeah, totally," and grabbed it off the guitar stand in my office and played a song for her. It was probably "I'll Believe in Anything" by Wolf Parade; I'd put together an acoustic arrangement of that that I like quite a lot. It's nice. It's comfy. She chopped quietly and listened, tearing up because she was so wound up by waking up at four in the morning to make Thanksgiving food for her whole family and stressed out about work. She later told me that I made her feel special and cared for and brought her some peace, and that that was the criteria she measured men by when she was thinking about new relationships now—that they could bring her that feeling.

That call is one of three memories I can easily access from the second half of 2020: that, camping with my partner's family, and Christmas dinner with mine. It was a hard year, and the rest of it is very blank in my mind.

THE BLOB

Maybe we could all go back to that morning together, and you could sit at the table with us while Hannah chops away and I noodle on my guitar. If you're comfortable with it, we'd like you to understand why she left F2K the first time.

It's easy to get distracted from the tremendous and horrifying things which we experience in our lives. We bury them beneath the daily grind, hidden in distant corners of our minds which we don't visit often. But the story of a pregnancy—all the emotions and pain and love and heartbreak—should be told, not hidden.

In college—during my first failed attempt to get a degree—I took an elective on United States childbirth culture which turned out to be the most memorable class of the first three years I was in school.

The class was taught by two doulas, both named Jane, and full of family-inclined young women, a female nurse, and myself. I was a bit of an outsider and even felt like a couple of the guest lecturers were treating me with hostility, but I loved the course. The day we experimented with pain control, I expressed that the chocolate didn't really work for me. Everyone else found that funny.

I've always been a storyteller. In high school, I was attracted to journalism—the search for truth and the ethical ways in which it should be told—and in college, I studied all manner of stories, whether that meant putting together statistical analyses of the structure of the deaths told of in the *Iliad*, reading about the conferences and figureheads that were instrumental in developing the scientific method, or listening to the details women had to share about the births of their children. My main takeaways from this class were that stories about pregnancy and birth are incredible, and that every mother has one, and that they are full of raw emotion and joy and pain, and that they are worth listening to, even worth asking about. When friends of mine had their first children, I started to ask what the pregnancy and birth had been like and loved hearing what they had to say and sharing in their animated emotions.

My mother's mother used to love telling the story of the first time she saw me. My mum was still in her hospital bed, and I was bundled up in a blanket. My grandmother picked me up, and I opened my big blue eyes and looked up at her, and she fell in love. That's the entire story, and I've heard it thousands of times. Every time she met one of my new friends, every time we were relaxing in the evening, every time I was upset, she told that story one more time. It was one of our rituals. It feels right that I'd want to know other stories about birth, too.

***

At the beginning of 2019, right after I'd joined F2K, Hannah started waking up at 4 a.m. to pee every morning. After a few days, she bought a pregnancy test without her boyfriend, Jake, knowing. The next morning she woke up at 4 a.m. again and brought the test with her to the bathroom. It was positive. She went back to bed and lay awake for hours, churning through everything in her head, waiting for Jake to wake up so she could tell him. Hannah can get anxious sometimes, and she cares about others more than herself. She found herself worrying about whether she was failing the other people at her job, getting overwhelmed imagining all the stress that a pregnancy would entail, and feeling afraid of giving birth.

When Jake woke up, he responded just how she needed him to. He is protective of the people he loves, and he spent three days reading all about pregnancy and working out all the things he could do to help. At work she told Mat and Aleks, her two longest-term co-workers from all the way back when F2K came in to help Good Gaming, and they began affectionately referring to her baby as "The Blob." She told her mother, but her mother was preparing to leave to go to Korea to be with other relatives, so the conversation was bittersweet. Her parents are still married, but they've found that their relationship works a lot better if they live in different countries. Hannah reminded me that there are all sorts of traditional things which Korean women do for each other to help with pregnancy—for example, cooking a type of seaweed soup which is high in iron to help keep the body healthy and give the baby lots of nutrients. She had moved to Alabama to help her cousin with this once, but now there was no one around to do it for her.

Hannah is five feet four. She has long, dark hair, and tattoos of flowers on her arms. I can picture her standing at the chopping board, telling me over the phone: "I told her I'd be okay, because I'm always okay."

At Hannah's first appointment with a doctor, everything was normal, but the next time she visited, everything was not. She was concerned because she'd had some bleeding; the nurse told her that this might be normal, or it might not, and proceeded to run some tests. Later that day, the nurse called her and carefully explained that the hormone level they were measuring should have doubled between visits, but instead it had dropped. It was the first indicator of a miscarriage.

Hannah sat on the other end of the line, unable to respond, and began to sob, her heart shattering in ways she still can't explain today. When she could finally say something, her first words were an apology. Already her thoughts were fixing on empathy for the nurse, who had to tell women this sort of news all the time. In my memory, I can hear the pleading in her tone as she recounts having asked, "Is there still a possibility?" But there wasn't.

Her mother was on the way to the airport when she picked up the phone, and there was no way she could stay. She told Hannah not to cry, and to eat the seaweed soup because it was still good to have during a miscarriage.

Hannah went to a follow-up appointment to go through her options with her gynecologist. The doctor said Hannah's body should "naturally expel"—the grimacing quotation marks are audible in her speech—the baby. She had a choice between taking a pill for this immediately or waiting a week first in case the pill was unneeded. She chose to wait a week, which turned out to be full of bleeding and pain. She went to the doctor again, and he suggested that she should take the pill, as it was taking too long. So she took the pill, but it didn't work. There was more bleeding and pain. She was given Vicodin for the pain and had a vasovagal response to it. She felt like throwing up and going to the bathroom at the same time; her heart started beating weirdly, erratic and out of place. She walked to the bathroom and looked at herself in the mirror to find that her face was completely devoid of any color, lips grey and clammy from the cold sweat. She sat on the toilet and tried to control her breathing. She felt like she was going to faint but tried to focus on breathing until she could feel her heart beating normally again. Jake came in, knowing something was wrong; she could tell from how terrified he looked that this wasn't right.

Five days later, she went to the bathroom and found parts of her Blob on her pad. It was gory. It was traumatizing. She sat, staring at the bloody remnants of her child, crying silently so Jake wouldn't hear her. Eventually she gently folded up the pad, wrapped it in layers and layers of tissue paper, and placed it in the trash can. She didn't talk about this with Jake. She didn't talk about this with anyone, and nobody asked if she needed to.

Hannah is the most selfless and kind person I've ever met, but she has spent her life in strategy gaming. The young men she knew didn't understand what she was going through. As she processed her loss over the next few days, she started getting angry about everything. She found herself becoming irritable and resentful. She couldn't handle going out in public; she couldn't handle seeing people with their kids. And even though the pill had worked partially, there was still more of the Blob in her womb. After everything she'd endured, she would have to go through surgery anyway.[45] Her resentment grew and grew, taking its place in the hole in her chest where her love had been. All she wanted to do was love her child, but it was gone. All she wanted from others was for them to acknowledge her grief, but they ignored it.

She even stopped talking with Jake. One of the things she's realized since is that pregnancy loss can be almost as hard for fathers as it is for mothers. While her support network wasn't enough, Jake's was non-existent. He had no guy friends he could turn to who would understand what he was going through at all. She didn't realize it at the time, but he'd been staying up with her each night, supporting her while she cried herself to sleep—and only then would he start crying himself. They eventually got into a huge argument about nothing in particular and both ended up in tears. After that, she was angry with herself, too. She felt like something was wrong with her.

---

45 A couple of years later, the United States Supreme Court struck down Roe v. Wade's protection of abortions, and I found myself reading articles about women in Hannah's situation who were denied the sorts of care her doctor had given her and left to struggle on without them—or travel to other states or countries where they were legally protected. Shame. Shame on us.

Even though Hannah had left F2K after her demotion and the news of her pregnancy, John had kept calling her all the time; he had a tendency to unload on certain people emotionally without considering their service to be a form of work, and didn't see why he should stop using Hannah for that even though she'd left the company. He'd been bragging about good things that were happening with F2K because of a new business relationship they were forming. He had finally been able to give salary raises to himself and staff. Eventually he called from Tyson Ranch to tell her he'd been meeting streamers from the team and even Mike Tyson himself. On one of these calls, Hannah told him that she'd had a miscarriage, and when he heard that her baby was dead, he started wanting her back at F2K again.

Later, he jokingly asked if she was planning to get pregnant again anytime soon, in a conversation with her about whether she would be able to be fully committed to the job. She didn't speak to him for two months. In fact, she pretty much didn't speak to anyone. Her mother wasn't in the country; her sister-in-law knew about the miscarriage but never reached out. The one thing she could've used most was someone sending her a message or calling her on the phone and asking her if she was okay. Nobody did. When I realized this later, I felt like I'd failed her—she'd worked for me this entire time, and I never asked.

One of the ways in which my friendship with Hannah is deficient is that she doesn't ask for help because she doesn't want to impose on other people, and I don't ask people if something's wrong because I don't want to pry into their lives, and so sometimes we pass each other in the night when we should be helping each other. I only learned how to ask for help properly a few years ago—maybe the most important thing I've ever learned; if you don't ask people for help regularly, you should really try it—and maybe my next goal should be to get better at recognizing when I should be offering it.

After a couple of months, in late 2019, Hannah started to worry about money. She also hated going out into the world for her "regular" job—doing inventory and invoicing at a warehouse. So, she told John she was willing to come back to F2K. (Her warehouse job was an hour commute each way, and when I asked her what it had been like, she said "BORING" in a voice which should be written in all caps. I wasn't surprised. She is brilliant and incredible with people and built for the streaming world, for putting out fires nobody has ever seen before and reassuring streamers who are upset about things nobody else has ever dealt with.) We agreed that she'd keep working for me as well, and she rejoined the team as a talent manager.

Hannah and Jake still live together. They've supported each other through the coronavirus pandemic; they have a couple of dogs. But something about their relationship broke during the miscarriage and won't ever come back. She says that she likes that they live together, that it's like living with her best friend, but I can almost feel myself suffocating when I imagine how much happier they could have been together, raising a child. The only time that Hannah mentions her father in this story is to say that he thinks she'd be a good mom, which is one of the most succinct and truthful things I've ever heard. But sometimes good things with the potential to be everything turn out bad and leave you broken.

***

It's possible that the story of Hannah's pregnancy is also the entire story of F2K. I could argue that the company's success was largely based on tremendous amounts of labor from her and a couple of other people, and the start of its death spiral lines up closely with the first time that she left the team. Such an argument would be incomplete and wouldn't quite do justice to the complexity and depth of F2K's failures, but it would be a great story.

Categorizations of our life detract from it. If you decide a part of the human experience is something lesser, you lose any hope of being able to truly understand it. Any time you experience anything as a human, you are experiencing life, and everything which happens in your life affects all other parts of your life. A common way to categorize life is to place some of it in a basket called "work," and some in a basket called "life," and talk about balancing the two, but there is no real work-life balance; the concept is an oversimplification. When you work, you are a human, and when you are at home, you are a human; you don't become some different being with different needs when you are at work, and then go home in the evening with the ability to isolate all of the experiences and traumas of the day in a separate compartment from your home life.

We lie to ourselves about this all the time. The reason it's compelling when an employer claims that their company is like a family is that the company is, in fact, like a family. If you spend all day working with the same people and grow to trust and understand them, that is real human interaction. There might be hatred; there might be love; there might be anything in between. Of course, then the employer might pull the rug out from under your feet. Perhaps they don't actually care about you, you get fired, and they forget about you immediately. When people exploit us through the very real and human connections which we hold to be important, they can cause immense misery.

Maybe Hannah isn't a mother, but when she speaks about her pregnancy, she certainly sounds like one. When she talks about her dogs, she sounds like a mother. When she cares about other people and loves other people, she does so in the way a mother might. It's easy to listen to her words and hear that she is experiencing the grief of a mother losing her child. The second that she saw her positive test result and told Jake she was pregnant, they started to become parents, and Hannah's miscarriage didn't erase that. They are still parents—they are just parents who lost their child. This might not be how pregnancy loss works for everyone else, but when you listen to Hannah's story, it is obvious that it is how it worked for her. It is a story of lost potential, deeply worth acknowledging.

Second by far to Hannah's loss, but still significant, is the loss of her story—the fact that she felt silenced and ignored as she dealt with emotions which could have connected her to the people around her instead of making her resent them. She had been working in gaming for five years, but almost none of her friends could relate to her experience in any way. Her boss reframed it as a joke about getting her to work harder for him, and her guy friends had no idea what to say. She didn't have any female friends in this space, and there are almost no mother figures here.

Online gaming as it exists now is perhaps twenty years old, and the demographics of the space reflect that; as a thirty-five-year-old I am regularly the oldest person in a group. Hannah's experience is a symptom of the space's horrifically skewed demographics, and this is a problem worth fixing. A world without elders—defined by men in their thirties working to exploit men in their twenties—cannot be healthy.

THE STORM

C ome with me to 2021 now, a year later. I am taking a night off from writing this memoir to watch a new comedy special. I'm tired of writing. I'm tired of corroborating stories, of reaching out to women to ask them if they'd be interested in talking to me about some rumors of sexual impropriety that I'd heard. I don't want to analyze and criticize humans—I want to live in a neighborhood with them. I don't want to ask people to confirm their past traumas for me. I've made a book full of the traumas of myself and my friends, and I don't want to open it to edit it anymore—I want to throw it into the deepest hole on Earth, and will it to never have been real.

John used to tell me that, when we got older, he wanted everyone to move onto the same street together, and he'd grill dinner on the barbecue and we'd all hang out. I want that. Or I want to live back in that innocent world where I once wanted it.

When Wirtual released his report on cheating in *Trackmania*, which ended Riolu's streaming and content creation career— instantly vanished him off the Internet—he spoke a lot about how difficult working on the report had been for him. His job wasn't to be the *Trackmania* police; he was just a content creator and entertainer who played the game. He'd spent months working on the report, carefully trying to work out the right ways to release it to give the people accused of cheating the best possible chance to save face, all while he was working full-time at his day job as a content creator, streaming to thousands of people and publishing YouTube videos to millions. And when he did release it, making himself the bearer of bad news, many people blamed him for the fact that they could no longer enjoy Riolu's entertaining (if manipulative) content.

I empathize with Wirtual so much. I don't feel like it should be my job to write the things I'm writing. I've always felt like it would be cool to publish a book, but I never wanted it to be about this. As I read my drafts, I find myself wondering where the hero of the story is. The hotshot lawyer, who works pro-bono to win Hannah millions of dollars in a sexual harassment case, setting a precedent protecting women in this industry for years to come. Or the muckraking journalist, who wins national attention with a damning exposé in a noteworthy magazine. I'm just a guy. I stream video games. Sometimes I struggle to believe I'm doing anything good at all, and wonder if I'm just a narcissist who wants to talk about himself.

I watch this comedy special and it isn't funny. Bo Burnham has spent a year in a room through the pandemic and basically recorded, produced, and published his own mental breakdown. I read peoples' reactions to it. They're talking about how fucked-up it is. About how he sat on his own in a room for a year and created something entrancingly unpleasant. How hard it is for them to watch. How they take some sort of sadistic pleasure from watching it again with friends who haven't seen it yet, and seeing their reactions. But when I watch it, I just think, "Yup." I think, "That seems familiar." I think about a year and a half spent entertaining people through a pandemic, and about the book I'm writing. I rewatch it a couple of times. I start judging my mental state largely by which of Burnham's new songs are repeating in my head.

I love the essays of David Foster Wallace, but they are one of the saddest things in the world to me. He was such a genius, and for each essay he would spend a few weeks or months learning about something new and then beautifully put in words the central reasons why it was terrible and heartbreaking—and then, after a career of doing that over and over again, he killed himself. In my head, my narrative insists that maybe if he hadn't just been an essayist, he could have changed things. Maybe if he'd spent his life advocating for lobster welfare, he could have fixed how humans consumed lobster, instead of just writing a haunting essay about how wrong it was. Maybe then he would have been happy. Maybe he could have been happy if he'd spent his life the way that I'm spending my life on strategy games. I have to believe that, because I want that to be true about myself. I don't want to yell complex thoughts into a void to no effect. I don't want to kill myself ten years from now.

But I wake up some mornings and don't really want to be alive, either. I don't want to die—I want to spend every moment I have on helping people. I am a boat. I slog onward through the waves. It's just, do I have to be conscious for it all? Do I have to be here? I can't scream because it'll peak my microphone—an instinct I can't seem to turn off, even though I know my stream isn't live. I'm sure that, if I scream, someone who has fallen asleep to my voice will wake up in shock. I can barely breathe—if I hyperventilate, it will be too loud. I must be calm. I am a boat.

I want to revisit the tone of the book and add more levity—balance it out. But that's out of a misguided sense of responsibility toward you, to shelter you from harm and negativity. This is a moment for me to be vulnerable; to tell you about my conflicts, not protect you from them. And so here I am at five in the morning, still awake, but I can't scream or my mic will peak. *I can't scream*. My mic will peak.

***

When my grandfather on my mother's side was in his twenties, he was diagnosed with bipolar disorder. He spent fifty years on lithium, slowly developed Parkinson's symptoms as a side effect, and was in and out of mental wards for his last twenty. Bipolar disorder is scary in the streaming community. A huge figurehead of streaming, Reckful—one of the first big names of my profession—killed himself in July 2020, at age 31, after his own prolonged battle with it. When I asked a friend who was close to him if she had anything she would like to say, she told me that she wished she did, but that when she thought about it, it was like her brain turned into a storm. I think she actually said a lot. So many of us know that storm.

Bipolar disorder is genetic. I think it lurks in my brain somewhere, but I think I keep it under control. I don't drink anymore, and other than alcohol, I've spent my entire life avoiding any substance that I think might fuck up my brain, because I know that it can take a long time for it to right itself again. At some point I noticed that if I spent a night drinking, I would feel depressed three days later.

I just want to be surrounded by people who care about me, and whom I can care about in the same way. I want to be respected, not because I'm a world-class strategy gamer but because I'm a human being. I want to be understood. I want to believe that there are women in the world who love games and haven't been fucked up because of it and that I can find one of them to be happy with, but I don't think it is okay for me to want that. It's unfair to my last partner, who tried to play games with me and stopped when she was made fun of in her first ever game online with other people. It's unfair to myself, to believe that anything like that will ever be that easy for me again. And it feels unfair to other women, too. Another selfish request. Another man asking them to be something for him.

I lost touch with reality one night, when I was 18. A guy on an online forum I used to post on was making fun of me, and I handled it badly, and then other people poked at me for handling it badly, and I spent four hours making spreadsheets of their online activity, fully convinced that all of the other accounts making fun of me were controlled by the same guy, repeatedly logging in as a new persona to hurl another insult at me. But I woke up in the morning and I was okay. My grandfather didn't always wake up like that the next morning. He spent his final years sitting on his bed in his assisted living facility, going through his files, convinced he was uncovering a plot by the staff at the facility to kill him. My sister didn't, two years ago, and spent two weeks in a mental ward. I want to hug her and shelter her entire body like I could when she was a baby. My parents left her alone for a few minutes, on the bed in her carrier, when they first brought her home from the hospital. I was eight, and I noticed she was alone and watched over her, and one of the reasons that I need to stay sane is that I'm still not ready to stop.

When my grandfather had breakdowns, I was the only person he would trust. Not nurses, not his wife, not his children. Just his eldest grandchild, who had played board games on the floor while he read his Bible. His blue-eyed grandson who came back home to New Zealand to try playing online poker, because he couldn't in the States, and spent most of the time sitting in a chair watching cricket with him in silence instead, because poker was boring, and spending time with him was more important, and we both already knew everything that there was to say.

He would walk to the furthest possible point he could, every time we said goodbye. To the bus stop, where he waited in the rain, and hugged me as I left. To the parking lot of the assisted living facility, hobbling, struggling to stand up straight and wave and be strong. When his own mother had gotten old, he had built a small unit out back of his house for her, and looked after her, and sometimes she got grumpy with him for leaving divots in the grass when he played soccer or rugby with me—and then my family went overseas and put him in a retirement home.

One afternoon, we got a call from the mental ward. I was in the States, so far away, and he was far away, too, in his own way. Most of him was hiding deep in a corner of his brain, sheltered from the world. The part I got to talk to told me he had something important to say, but he couldn't say it out loud on the phone because he thought they might be monitoring his phone calls, so he asked me if I was getting his message in my mind. I told him I wasn't. He seemed surprised, but was resolute. He asked, "Does this help?" and started reciting numbers, slowly and deliberately so that I could hear them. Lovingly. It didn't help.

When I visited him in the ward with my family one time, I got frustrated that he wasn't as good at playing canasta as he used to be. He used to be brilliant, but that day he wasn't there. He was doing the math wrong, and not understanding whose turn it was. I couldn't handle his being gone. I needed to lose myself in the game we were playing, but I couldn't get lost because he kept on forgetting the rules.

When my grandmother died, I had tried to make it home for her, but the flight took too long. Too many people met me at the airport. I spent a week surrounded by family I barely knew and got upset at the woman who tried to sell us an expensive coffin. I didn't bother trying to make it home when my grandfather died. I was broken at the time; I couldn't do it.

***

I don't think I can receive messages with my mind, or send you any. I'm mostly okay, I think. But I can time travel, and maybe just this once, you can come with me, if you promise not to tell anybody. There was this one time I got pizza at a corner store in Italy. Here, I'll show you. We should go quietly—I don't want to peak the mic.

The central character of my past is the storm. It is the same storm you know in the present. It breaks against my hull—I am a boat which floats beside you as you walk down the street. It is raining in a way that does not pour because the rain does not go down; it stays all around you. Rain bounces off the pavement and soaks your waist in water underneath your coat. You are walking in the rain carrying a guitar and two backpacks because you did not buy a map and cannot read Italian, and because you are fleeing a dead relationship and the inside of the storm provides refuge. Is it okay for your abusive ex to show up with her apologetic mother and brother the day after the breakup saying she'd left something behind and then leave at a brisk walk carrying one of the cats? It was your least favorite of the cats but you did still quite like it and you feel like the cats relied on each other.

It is my fault, the storm, because my weight and volume displace water and I am heavy and large. I am a boat, struggling against the tide. But the storm makes it easier to grip things somehow—the handle of the guitar case swells with rainwater— and you're only walking anyway. It's mostly okay. It is a fact of life: How could there be anything else which was better or worse?

We go inside the first door that looks commercial. It is a corner store. You are dripping with water and the insides of the store are . . . dry? The water must come through the door, the cracks in the windows. At any moment, it will collapse the roof, or it will well up from the pipes beneath us.

You try to set your dripping belongings in the corner of the store and you look miserable, which the shopkeeper mistakes for looking apologetic because of cultural differences. The word for pizza in Italian is "pizza" and you can choose toppings by pointing at which slice you want. You communicate that you do not want it heated up, which may not have been what you wanted to communicate. You are in a stage of your life where you are "trying new things" and smiling. You have just spent a week passing through Boston on the way to this month in Europe. You have no plans while you're here, no, but in Boston you were going to visit two people and walk the Freedom Trail in a thunderstorm (a different storm which was the same storm and which was unplanned but in retrospect obvious). You don't even need to reinvent yourself; you are just the type of person who would spend some time in Europe with no plans, no job, no . . .

The pizza arrives. Despite not being the sort of person who needs to reinvent yourself, you have asked for the one with potato and broccoli on it. It is. And the storm is not, for a moment.

***

Are you dizzy? Are you okay? We are back. Sometimes I have to go there, to eat the pizza again. I need it every day, I think, but I can't eat it here. I shouldn't eat on camera: It grosses people out, and if I turn my camera off and mute my microphone, I will lose viewers.

CORPORATE MANAGEMENT

Toward the end of 2020, Oliver (from Rally) joined F2K as co-CEO to try to tidy the team up for investment potential with his professional (and very San Francisco, USA) approach. He had a tendency to namedrop people, which is one of the ways you knew he was the real deal, although he kept namedropping how he'd worked with Pokimane, the most successful woman on Twitch, and like, while she is incredible, I had been playing *Among Us* with her every now and then, and couldn't help but notice that I had not been put in charge of the company. (She never mentioned him.)

Oliver brought a couple of "professionals" with him, and they legally moved the company from Guernsey to the US[46] and started implementing some changes. Will, one of the three main new guys (they were all male), took over talent management, becoming Hannah's new boss. He had been an influencer manager for Disney's presence in Asia and told stories about how he'd been chewed out by his bosses for not seeking exclusively to maximize their profit margins, and how it had made him feel bad.

While I had sympathy for the story, I also had equity in the company, giving me full access to our financials whenever I'd like, and my sympathy ran out rapidly when I found out the three of them were each being paid more than a hundred thousand dollars

---

46   Specifically Delaware, I think? Although if I remember right our contract disputes were meant to be settled in California. It all seemed confusing and laughably irrelevant to me, but I'm sure it was the sort of thing which might mean a lot to investors.

per year. None of them knew how F2K worked, and while they all had experience in professional spaces which sort of related to what F2K was, none of them had actual experience at a company like F2K.

As one of the streamers with an interest in backend stuff, I did a good chunk of unpaid labor trying to get the new guys up to speed. I got trotted out for a panel with investors, where I felt the new staff performed somewhat admirably in sounding like they had passion and knowledge about the space. I spent an hour or so on a call with Will, trying to explain to him that his pledges to do right by the talent and to always be on our side in disputes didn't mean anything to me. They weren't things he could follow through on, given his job title and the structure of our business relationship, but he continued to earnestly pledge that he'd be on my "side." This was another moment when I had to wonder: ignorant, or feigning ignorance?

At first, the structure of the company did seem to be changing, and there were some reasons to have hope—but there were also a lot of red flags.

We started having monthly conference calls where the streamers tuned in to watch presentations and hear introductions and so forth. A chance to hear the life stories of the staff, or to hear what F2K stood for. These were a cute idea.

The problem was that most of us didn't care very much. We were contractors who were using F2K to secure sponsorships for ourselves, and most of us had given up on the idea that we were part of a powerful team brand worth caring about sometime during the first month of the Softgiving sponsorship. The company hadn't given us reason to believe that anything had changed; the new staff were simply asking us to start believing in that team brand again for what felt like no reason.

We were also better at the things we were watching the presentations on than the people who were giving the presentations. I'd spent six years working out how to navigate subjects like sexism and racism in front of an audience of thousands of people, been vetted and tested enough as a streamer to make partner on Twitch, and been vetted and tested enough to be signed and salaried and given equity in F2K, and I didn't appreciate being told I had to make space in my sixty-plus-hour workweek to watch a corporate presentation on how I shouldn't be racist because it was against F2K's values. No shit. It was against F2K's values when they'd vetted me and signed me to the team as well. Also, F2K's values had no relevance as to whether or not we should be racist; we shouldn't be racist no matter what F2K thought.

Even more awkward was that a lot of this sort of stuff was ham-handedly angled at streamers who were relevant because they pushed back against rules like the ones being covered in the presentations. What was the point of signing the most openly progressive *Magic: The Gathering* streamer in the world and then asking him to sit through a presentation on the way the company thought we should treat all political viewpoints with respect?

Plus we were even better at giving presentations, than them. I have a good friend from high school who does theater, and whenever I go to his parties, I quiet down a lot and enjoy myself because everyone else there is better at commanding a room and animating physical space than I am. F2K was trying to run sixty-minute live shows for an audience of thirty streamers who had each basically been rolling out of bed and livestreaming for eight hours a day for the last five years. We could all do this better than they were, and I didn't have much patience for sitting through their fuck-ups.

An even bigger change was that we stopped individually negotiating sponsorship contracts with our managers at F2K. Instead, F2K tried to set up opt-in sponsorship categories. We answered a survey on our comfort level with advertising lots of different categories of things, like fast food, and if we said that we were comfortable, F2K automatically opted us into any incoming fast food sponsorship.

This idea failed because we ourselves were not fast food. We were, as they say, human beings. We wanted to negotiate different sponsorships based on rates, the exact brand (being okay with promoting free-range chicken didn't automatically mean someone was okay with promoting homophobic chicken), our schedule, the actual type of content we were being asked to make for the sponsorship, and so on and so forth. This was a little bit complicated, but the idea that F2K could get to know us and use their expertise to bring us the exact types of sponsorships that we desired, at good rates, had been the starting premise of the team's existence.

There was also a lot of ambiguity happening when it came to money. F2K stopped telling me how much they were being paid for the promotions I was doing, while at the same time expecting me to tell them whether I was okay with doing something or not. I am, as a general rule, not interested in promoting something if I am paid $0, and very interested in doing so if I am paid $100,000, and where things switch in the middle depends on my current financial status, energy, and the product in question. Part of the problem was that the so-called professionals we were paying a hundred thousand dollars a year weren't familiar with standard rates for sponsorships in the space and also somehow didn't know the standard rates that the streamers who had been on the team for two years were usually getting.

***

Back to Will, the new Talent Manager. As a person, Will was uninspiring. You know how stories with bad plots can be hilarious, and stories with great plots are engaging, but stories with a mediocre plot are just unworkable? Will came off as a story with a mediocre plot. He'd had one experience working for a big corporation in Asia, which didn't work out, and now he was—here I'm checking my notes again—paid $120,000 a year to provide assistance managing my streaming career.

Half of the problem was me, though, at that point. By then, I was broken. I couldn't talk to Will and believe that he was a good person. Too much had happened; the wires didn't connect anymore. I find it sort of strange that I feel bad about that; the company had a contract with me, and I fulfilled every clause of that contract fully for two and a half years, and yet I'm the one who feels like I'm broken because I didn't have much respect for one of the guys asking me to do extra unpaid work for him. Other people seemed to think he was fine, but I had run out of patience at this point.

Will spent a lot of time complaining to me about "professionalism"—I was one of the more responsive, agreeable, and articulate streamers, so he expected me to be on his side about this. He wanted streamers to get back to him quickly when he sent them messages, and tried to get forty-eight-hour response times into the new contracts. He generally wanted streamers to be on top of things and know what was going on. In a lengthy call, I tried to explain to him that that was the entire service that F2K was providing.

If streamers were on top of things and knew what was going on and were always able to respond about sponsorships within forty-eight hours, they could do all of the things that F2K did on their own. Doing these things for the streamers was the reason F2K got paid commission. Will said that, when push came to shove, he would rather build a team out of streamers who behaved professionally than the less professional ones. Later, when push came to shove, I told him that he'd need to offer me ten times as much money for me to sign the contract he'd offered because he was trying to get me to sign over a ton of things that I could manage on my own.

Speaking of which, one of the big tasks that Oliver and company were undertaking was to revamp our contracts. Previously, F2K had existed on contracts about five pages long which succinctly outlined the business relationship between the company and the streamer, but now we were going to get real, "professional" contracts with another fifteen pages of legalese. They had been working on them for a while before I finally got my first look at one.

Hannah let me know that Will wanted to start going over the new contracts with people and that he wanted to schedule a call with me to help me read through it. I told her I wasn't interested in reading assistance; if Will wanted to talk about a contract with me, he could send it over so I could read through it and write up feedback on it, which he did. I started reading through it and, after about a thousand words of notes, I rolled my eyes and decided I'd just wing it with him for the second half.

A fundamental misunderstanding that F2K seemed to have in presenting these contracts was a misjudgment of the relative importance of the two parties involved. For me, even with a decent number of sponsorship deals as a streamer, most contracts I've agreed to in my life have still been agreements between myself and some massive multinational corporation which were a hundred pages long and which I scrolled through without reading and clicked "accept" for at the end. This sort of contract makes sense when a billion-dollar corporation wants to protect itself legally, but the person signing has no actual skin in the game at all.

But now we were talking about my business signing a contract with F2K, and, not counting investment rounds, my business had an annual revenue within an order of magnitude of F2K's. Also, only one of us had a positive profit margin, and it wasn't F2K.

F2K's demands in the contract ranged from one-sided to insulting to thievery. They included a force majeure clause—a standard contractual element which forgives the parties for delivery of promised services in the event of a natural disaster—but it only applied to them. My feedback: "Hey Will, if you're going to add fifteen pages of legalese, I'd like them to protect me, too."

They wanted me to contractually opt in to a bunch of team-wide sponsorships without the right to even negotiate their terms. My previous contract had allowed full right of refusal for any sponsorship that I didn't want to participate in, because I'd signed my previous contract while F2K was not just in the gutter but halfway down the drain, and I didn't want them to force me into sponsorship deals that would ruin my channel.[47]

They wanted full control over the monetization of my YouTube channel and a significant cut of advertising revenue for sponsorships they brought to it. To me, this was the most ridiculous change. My YouTube channel gets around the same amount of traffic as my Twitch channel, and my previous contract had only allowed them to control parts of my Twitch channel. This paragraph alone, which Will seemed to think we'd glide over, would have been worth doubling my salary.

---

47 I had this clause in my contract and still agreed to run the Softgiving deal. I still wanted to work hard to help the team and stay on it! I just wanted to have the choice to say "no" if I needed to. In practice, John probably let me have that clause because he figured he could strong-arm me into anything he needed from me anyway, and he was right, but I liked having it in the contract, you know?

We had a one-sided discussion about the contract obligating team members to make [streamername]@f2k.gg email accounts, advertise them on all of their social media as their official email address, and give F2K full access to them. There were so many problems with this, and I went over them, one by one, while Will gave occasional grunts of acknowledgment.

There was the trust element, where fans think an email they send to me is going to be read by me, not a random member of staff. I've been getting people coming to me with personal problems and suicidal thoughts every week for the last three years, enough that I've spent time talking to professional counselors about crisis strategies, integrated support hotlines and channels into my community, and built a procedure for dealing with these sorts of communications in private. I didn't want those to be read by an F2K staffer.

There was the fact that my email represented me, and what happened after you sent an email to me reflected exactingly on who I was. I read my important emails, and Hannah handled the rest. It was a big enough job, in my opinion, that I had hired someone who exceled at it to improve my ability to fulfill it. I had no reason to believe F2K had the skill or motivation to do this task in a way which reflected well on me.

There was also the actual reason that F2K was asking for access to my email: They wanted to intercept the sponsorship deals which came directly into my email inbox, negotiate them for me, and potentially turn them into team-wide sponsorships. I did not want this at all. This was abhorrent to me. The contract even mandated that I disclose every sponsorship that I did to them. It was a complete reversal of the reason that I'd joined the team in the first place. I didn't want someone I barely trusted to be negotiating sponsorship deals that I was already getting offered; I wanted someone to bring me extra sponsorship deals that *weren't* already showing up in my email inbox.

It wouldn't even have worked. I couldn't just disclose all the sponsorships that I was doing to F2K and have them take them over. I have working relationships with sponsors which go back years now. They message me on Discord and Twitter, and we share gossip and chat about life, and slowly they learn what sorts of things I enjoy promoting on my channel. They are friends of mine who understand a different part of the industry from me and who can often find useful deals which match my channel exactly. Sometimes we meet up for a drink at a convention and they surface opportunities to me there. What these people are bringing to me couldn't fit neatly into a jorbs@f2k.gg email address.

Also, there was some weirdly puritanical stuff about inappropriate sexual attention in the code of conduct they wanted me to sign. I briefly explained to Will what consent was, as I couldn't actually tell whether or not the people who'd written the contract knew. You don't have to outlaw sexual attention; people like it sometimes, and the way to tell if it's okay or not has to do with whether they're giving informed and uncoerced consent. Oh, and they had a clause protecting political affiliation and sexual orientation in the same line, and I suggested maybe those shouldn't be treated equivalently. People hired to try to juice as much profit as they can out of a company probably shouldn't be writing the code of conduct.

They wanted me to sign this contract without increasing my salary, after a year in which I had temporarily taken equity instead of pay to keep the company from going under, the largest sponsor they'd managed to bring me had been a repulsive for-profit charity middleman, and the team had raised hundreds of thousands of dollars in investment money. I tried to explain to Will that this wasn't a contract I was interested in signing, and that if I were going to, he would need to add at least another zero to how much he was offering to pay me.

I think there are people in the world who came up through certain business programs or corporate backgrounds who are genuinely incapable of understanding that other humans can think and have agency, too. It's stunning to me that someone could present that contract to me and think that I was going to sign it, or anything close to it. But at the same time, it's probably how more than 99% of contract negotiations go. "Here's an incredibly insulting and one-sided contract. Sign it, and we will give you some money—maybe."

The starting premise of business and trade is that if I have something which you could benefit more from, and you have something which I could benefit more from, we can exchange the two things, and overall, we'll both be happier. In my opinion, a good businessperson is someone who is very good at finding and facilitating those trades. I think Hannah is a very good businessperson, for example, because she is better than anyone else I have ever met at taking a game developer who is making a game that would do well on my channel and organizing a sponsored deal with them in a way that makes both me and them happy. I think John was also, despite everything else, a good businessperson, because when things got tough, he got down into the mud and put in twelve-hour days booked wall-to-wall with calls to streamers and sponsors, managing to find sponsors who were barely worth taking to keep F2K alive and making concessions to streamers to make them feel okay about taking those sponsorships. Maybe his motivations were corrupt and his ideals were wrong, but he was damn good at facilitating business.

But as far as I can tell, this is not what is taught at business school or talked about in board and investor meetings, or at least not the ones full of men who have succeeded on the backend of the esports industry. Those conversations seem to be about how to make the most personal profit. They don't seek to make a deal which serves two parties; they seek to position their company in a way which exploits a market. They start with an interaction someone else has already found, which used to benefit both parties involved in it, and try to work out how to wring it dry, until they are the ones receiving as much of the benefit as possible.

I do not think these behaviors are the behaviors of good businesspeople. Other terms come to mind. I think dictators are good at exploiting a population. Monopolists, capitalists. I think this is a defining behavior of people who are exemplary at being selfish. "Assholes" suggests itself from somewhere in my mind. At some point in history, this behavior saw the vulnerable, fledgling concepts of trade and business and monopolized them for itself. This isn't just not good business: It is exactly the opposite of good business. Good business relies on mutual trust and respect.

The prisoner's dilemma is a common tableau from game theory which I've found applies here, as it does in many other places. It is a thought experiment in which two people, incapable of honest negotiation, will receive the best overall outcome if they choose to cooperate with each other, but each of them is individually best served by backstabbing the other. It's a perplexing problem. If the other person cooperates, defecting will increase your value because you will get to take advantage of them. If the other person defects, there was never any real possibility of benefitting from a mutual cooperation with them, so you're best served to defect as well, leaving yourself less vulnerable to harm. Either way, you're doing better for yourself—so how can we ever, acting as self-interested human beings, reach the best overall outcome, in which both parties cooperate?

One answer is "enforcers." It doesn't work as well to backstab the other person if you'll get run out of town by their friends afterwards. This aspect of the prisoner's dilemma has been studied in bats. Bat mothers feed young bats communally, but some try to defect, opting not to feed the young of other bats so as to keep more energy for themselves. Enforcers in the bat community punish those mothers by denying them food. I was left at a loss, observing that bats were better at this thing than the humans controlling the backend of my streaming career. I found myself wondering if I should just go out in the woods at night with a blank contract and see what happened.

I try to be an enforcer in my life at times—I don't just spend energy cooperating, I go out of my way to try to make sure others cooperate, too. Apparently sometimes I write a book about it.

You can also just . . . choose to cooperate. You don't have to be self-interested. A lot of modern economics and game theory starts with an assumption that humans are self-interested and, in doing so, normalizes inexcusable behavior that is a tremendous contributor to our current problems as a society. The assumption isn't meant to be true; it's just an easy way of analyzing systems, and it often gives useful answers. Some humans are selfish; some are kind. If you are an empowered individual—someone who has enough resources to survive comfortably and whom the world treats kindly—and you would like other people to respect you, it becomes your responsibility as an adult to start thinking about people other than yourself.

The problem that kept on coming up in negotiations and maneuvering with Will and Oliver, and with a lot of the sponsors and investors they were talking with, was that they were all defecting all the time. It seemed that was the standard mode of proceedings on the business side of the industry. But if everyone defects, you all die from the inefficiency. Contracts which you should be able to draft and sign in a day become a six-month process with lawyers involved. And the second you've mistreated me, you lose my interest in fulfilling my end of our deals to the fullest extent of my capabilities; instead of trying to make us both successful, I start doing whatever is best for myself and my community.

In contrast, I've found that successful streamers tend to cooperate a lot. We smile and say nice things about each other, even if we don't get along. We invite each other to events and swap our schedules around to make them work without asking for payment or even expecting to bank up goodwill.

When I reach out to unfamiliar streamers to ask for their help, they usually get back to me in a couple of hours with insights that would've taken me years to reach on my own and kindly check in on how I'm doing. We might all be a bunch of overworked weirdos who get on each other's nerves sometimes, but we exist in social circles which are strong enough to facilitate positive interactions in spite of that.

While businesspeople are judged based on who they can namedrop and how big their ideas are, and it's easy for them to scheme and lie and misbehave behind the scenes—or sometimes misbehave quite openly, in someone like Benji's case—streamers are judged based on video evidence of the best and worst moments in their entire careers. Every now and then, a viewer reaches out to mention that someone said something transphobic in my channel four years ago and I didn't correct them properly. Or a bad relationship surfaces, and everything explodes. Streamers disappear for a year after stories come up about a night where they got drunk and behaved inappropriately toward someone, and their attempts to return to the limelight are met with thousands of people who still remember, or hadn't heard about it before but just read about it on social media. I know that the things I say now will be judged by anyone who feels entitled to judge them, not just today, but also against the standards of the future. This doesn't necessarily mean that streamers can't keep streaming after they make a faux pas. Many do! But the Internet rarely forgets.

On the subject of defecting, during this time Will kept telling me that he'd been evaluating the value of advertising on my channel and thought he could get more money from sponsorships for me. Which was largely true, by the way; if he were good at it, he could have. Hannah got me $4.5K for a two-hour gig in the same month that F2K found me $2K for a three-hour one. But Will brought this belief into negotiations with sponsors as an unrefined target. Instead of a simple demand and acquiescence, our negotiations were lengthy back-and-forths where the sponsor he had connected to through the business world made a number of unusual and unreasonable requests of me, then Will fired back with unusual and baseless requests of his own. Streaming is a big new space, and many negotiators are trying to set the rules for themselves to maximize their own earnings, but in doing so they can fail to create the trades and relationships which consistently benefit both parties and the space as a whole. All Will had to do was say "Hey, your product looks cool. Stephen's general mode of advertising is [how I advertise]. That's what I can sell you for his channel. Are you interested at [my price]?" If he wanted to get me paid more than usual, he had to find a company which really wanted what I could provide, or a thing I was particularly good at providing which a company wanted to pay me for.

One result of this sort of behavior was that all sorts of bizarre sponsorships were getting shoved onto channels where they didn't belong. Case in point: I'd been dealing with a chronic skin condition and expressed that I had interest in advertising a skincare company because I liked their business model. You submitted pictures of your skin and answers to a questionnaire, and a dermatologist would build you a custom skincare routine and send you the products for it. It was an iteration on a fairly common idea that had been successful with other kinds of products—in fact, it was basically identical to the first sponsorship deal I'd ever signed, with a company which had applied the same model to dental hygiene.

But instead of understanding how I advertised and offering that to the company, Will started up a lengthy negotiation in which I was a pawn, and two other organizations were trying to decide how they wanted to use me. Will wanted me to edit together a two-minute endorsement that would run during one of my YouTube videos, but I don't edit videos and don't put advertising in my YouTube content—both things I told him multiple times. He wanted me to try the product and give a personal endorsement if I liked it, but I had my own dermatologist who'd already worked out a skincare routine for me.[48] I didn't want to mess around with another product, and I wasn't comfortable endorsing skincare products based on my anecdotal experience anyway. I'm a strategy gamer; my audience understands the difference between professional endorsement and anecdotes. If any of them don't, my desire is to explain it to them, not to try to capitalize on their misunderstanding with advertising.

Instead of backing off and hearing what I was saying, Will kept doubling down. He got minor concessions from the company which didn't address all of the things that I'd already explained were deal-breakers for me. I mentioned that if I were getting paid $10K a month, that would be the starting point for me to consider doing this, thinking it was a ludicrous number which would make him stop trying to make this work, and he said he could get me $5K and then came back to me with $2.5K. He insisted—leveraging our contractual working relationship— that I communicate with my personal dermatologist to get the go-ahead to try the skincare routine that this company had made for me, as though the fact that that would only take five minutes made it a reasonable ask, and I foolishly believed his insistence that this was a reasonable ask and part of my obligation to the team and did so, allowing the fiasco to go on.

---

48   One of my major accomplishments in the misery of 2020 was actually signing up for a doctor's appointment and eventually seeing a specialist dermatologist in early 2021.

In another conversation about professionalism, I tried to explain to Will that if I asked streamers to play in one of my *Among Us* lobbies, they'd all get back to me in thirty minutes, because that was a tremendously appealing thing to them, and that one of the reasons that streamers weren't responding to his messages quickly was that he kept wasting their time bringing them stuff that they didn't care about. I didn't quite go so far as mentioning to him that doing so wasn't very professional.

LOVE AND FRIENDSHIP, PART TWO

I find it a lot easier to forgive people for the ways they treat me than for the ways they treat Hannah. When people mistreat Hannah, they are almost instantly dead to me. She gets similarly upset when people mistreat me—there have been a couple of times where the final straw for her wasn't how someone had treated her for four years, but rather how she saw them treating me the first time they met me. We go to war for each other.

Hannah didn't like to use her name or any pictures of herself while working for F2K. She left her webcam off in calls and went by a gender-neutral online username. After everything I've written here about how women are treated in this space, and about how Hannah was treated in F2K meetings, I don't imagine I have to justify her decision.

Oliver didn't like that. He decided that if F2K was going to be a professional company, that meant they were going to use first names and would have video on for all their calls. Hannah's desire not to comply with this was, he decreed, "unprofessional." Oliver really liked to deem anything that he didn't like "unprofessional" and weed it out, and he did so to several of the foundational behaviors that F2K's limited success had been dependent upon. It all came down to professionalism, whatever that was. I think maybe it was a stand-in for "whatever investors who don't understand the space very well would like to see." Investors would, of course, be unwilling to accept the narrative that the company's success was largely based on the underpaid labor of a woman who at this point was unsurprised when she was sexually harassed by the men on staff, and that it might be important to provide her limited comforts where it was easy to do so.

***

Webcams for professional meetings are a bizarre concept to me. As a streamer, I work in an industry where almost everyone has an entire high-quality studio set up to bring their audio/visual presence to the world. The studio usually serves some other roles too—sometimes it's your bedroom, or it's where you chill out and play games. Mine is where I'm writing this book.

As I sit here, I'm surrounded by $10,000 or so of audio/visual equipment including a couple of dSLR cameras and two different microphone + mixer + USB-interface setups. The back wall of the room is a green screen, and the floor is covered in green exercise mat pads. The side wall—which gets picked up by my secondary camera—is covered in posters[49] and lit by smart lights which are integrated with my stream and flash different colors when events happen on my channel.

In front of me is a wall with lights for my face and cameras on it, and a couple of bookshelves: one to hold my PC, router, mixers, etc., and another with an open filing system for tax documents, medical records, and all that, along with my collection of books. The wall to my left is mostly taken up by my window, which is covered in blackout film and usually shut during my streams. The room is badly susceptible to heat in summer, and the window isn't particularly functional because the blinds melted and the frame warped during a heat wave. A small duct runs along the floor to

---

49   At the time of writing this sentence, I still had an F2K poster up. I have since realized I should probably take that down.

bring fresh and cold air to my chair from an intake fan which is far enough away to not be picked up on my microphone.

In the beginning of 2020, I had a professional decluttering consultant spend a day helping me to donate books I didn't want anymore, get rid of that box of spare computer cables everyone has, set up a sensible filing system, and turn the closet space into functional storage for things I never used, like the printer.

This sort of setup isn't unusual for a streamer. Some forgo the webcam—or, in very few cases, even the microphone—and many don't have a dedicated room for their stream or haven't spent as much time structuring it, but most have put a lot of time and effort into creating a deliberate appearance for themselves to put out into the world.

Despite this, I have very rarely had business calls with other streamers where either of us have thought it was a good idea to turn our webcam on. It just isn't a thing which we think would be useful. There are all sorts of problems with it. Being on camera is uncomfortable, and we want to be comfortable while we come up with plans and discuss ideas together. Having someone look into your personal space during work feels like a breach of privacy, even if the space is shown off on stream every day while you're working. The lights strain our eyes. Seeing our own webcam feed in the video chat application is distracting. Particularly for women, it's nice not to feel pressure to look your best all the time.[50] Particularly for women, it can be nice not to wonder if the other person is fantasizing about your appearance instead of listening to your words—or at least to know that you're doing as little as possible to encourage them.

I use my presence on camera to lie to people. I don't mean that in a negative way; I mean that I've deliberately constructed

---

50 If I ever run an office and tell women that they have to dress or look a certain way, please fire me out of a cannon and into the sun.

the way I present myself to communicate the story that I am professional and calming and confident. The story isn't necessarily false, but the way that my presence on camera works is an attempt to highlight these characteristics. It looks authentic but really isn't very authentic at all. The only times I turn my camera on outside of the streaming part of my workday are for *D&D* games with very good friends or for calls with relatives whom I desperately want to see because I love and miss them. Oh, and for video counseling, which I think is a silly practice, but which I respect because my therapist says it's important and it doesn't seem worthwhile to spend a session challenging that. (Although, reading these paragraphs, I wonder if there might actually be some stuff to unpack.)

When I see other people on camera, I, similarly, feel like they're lying to me a little. Will had a bad green screen setup, and I spent a lot of our cam-on meetings distracted by it. Don't try to do the things that the people you work with are world-class at. Even if someone's webcam appearance isn't immediately jarring, the experience makes me think of newscasters or other entertainers—people who are telling me a story rather than trusted companions.

Meanwhile, my presence in an audio-only call feels truthful and vulnerable. That is how I have always called home to my parents or grandparents. It's how I kept up with friends as a kid and how I fell asleep listening to my girlfriend snoring softly on the other end of the line as a teenager and young adult. Maybe it's just a generational difference, but I'm still younger than a lot of the people who keep on telling me they want me to turn my camera on.

It bugs me that so much of the business world has decided that video calls are a good idea during work-from-home in this pandemic. Maybe they *are* a good idea, if the business world is based on lies and manipulation; I don't know. It seems like someone could have asked the people who talk to an audience on camera forty hours a week what they thought about this, but that never happened, and instead when I call up an old friend (audio-only) he tells me that he's starting to feel like he can empathize with my exhaustion from being on camera a little bit, and mentions that at his work they talk about "Zoom fatigue."

***

When Oliver joined the company as co-CEO, it was with the intention that he would take care of responsibilities back at the F2K base, while John was out trying to secure sponsors. There were parallels between this arrangement and the schism back when I'd first started with F2K, when John and Hannah had divvied up their responsibilities as CEO and COO based on John's interest in talking to strangers and Hannah's skill at keeping all the streamer stuff under control. Of course, at this time, Hannah was back at the company and could still have been managing those responsibilities, but she hadn't exactly risen through the ranks over the previous years. When Hannah *had* been handling that job, John had found it barely worth the position of COO. After her demotion at the beginning of 2019, she was only ever rehired in lower positions at the company.

Oliver's management style was obsequious. I actually have no idea what he did other than spend money and undo things which had already been working. He never spoke to me one-on-one, other than in our Rally Coin call before he even joined the company. I would describe Hannah's conversational style as empathetic, John's as diplomatic, Will's as sympathetic, and Oliver's as lizard person. There was always a three second pause between him hearing what you had to say and his response. For a lot of people, I would interpret that to mean they were thinking about what I'd just said, but with Oliver, it seemed like he was performing a medium-depth calculation as to which words would maximize his personal profit.

Around this time, FilthyRobot—the streamer who had taught me the ropes of streaming, and bonded with me over our mutual struggles with F2K—honestly and openly voiced some of his concerns about the company to John. His concise, bulleted list included bad sponsorships, a lack of communication, and worthless team meetings. John chatted with him for a while but let him know that Oliver was the one making those decisions; he would bring it up with Oliver and try to set up a conversation between the two of them.

When Oliver heard about my friend's complaint, he:

1. Preempted it by claiming he could already guess what it was going to be. (He was wrong.)

2. Said it didn't matter what my friend thought because he had a small channel. (Wow.)

3. Upon having both of those things corrected, said it wasn't worth talking to him because there was nothing he could do about it.

John's management style here—the one that had successfully kept me and Filthy with the team through a bunch of nonsense and under which we'd both worked for equity for several months—was to listen to our feedback, tell us he was going to do something about it, and then try to do something about it. I think in my last year there he increasingly didn't try very hard, but at least he claimed to be making some effort. This built trust and reliance and held the team together. It also allowed him to exploit us and get away with it. Oliver didn't do any of that; he just tried to exploit us and expected us to convince ourselves that it was okay on our own.

Oliver's success with cryptocurrency had been enough to bring him a CEO position for a moderately large team. Not that he was necessarily responsible for that success. Ethereum prices had gone up by an order of magnitude over the period of time I'm talking about. F2K was not similarly skyrocketing—it needed someone competent at the controls.

While Oliver was telling Hannah to turn on her webcam, Will was also keen to change her behavior. He told her how she should talk to streamers and sponsors, despite having perhaps a third of her experience, and being much worse at it than she was. Whenever she didn't follow the prescribed formula, he called her unprofessional and talked down to her. He and Oliver made her feel dumb, unqualified, and unvalued at a company that had succeeded largely due to her talent and four years of her hard work. She made one mistake with an email to a sponsor, which was largely the fault of instructions from people higher up in the company, and—echoing back to Pathra's time in competitive *Hearthstone*—was chewed out and ridiculed. She sometimes got scolded for going outside during the day.

She was also still in and out of her abusive relationship with one of the streamers on the team. She had broken up with him (for real now, after several failed attempts), and the situation had been escalated to John a while ago, with John giving the streamer a slap on the wrist over a moment when their personal disagreements had crossed over into their work relationship. But, inexplicably, Hannah was still in charge of managing her ex's sponsorships. Up until 2021, he had behaved during work calls, but while Oliver and Will were changing so much at the company, he acted out in one, and tensions flared up again.

Hannah asked Will if the streamer could be assigned to one of the other staff members on the team, and Will asked why. She explained that they'd had a rocky past and that it had come up in the workplace, and then Will asked to see the chat logs. He didn't just ask for the chat logs of this incident; he asked more generally for the chat logs from their relationship over the past year, an incredible breach of their privacy.[51] He wanted to determine who had initiated the relationship, and whether he thought it had been done inappropriately.

Word on the street here was that Will had developed a thing for Hannah, and he was about to do a little bit of white knighting. The first time I heard about all this, I'd found it almost comical, a last vestige of enjoyment from schadenfreude, but writing about it now, knowing everything else that had been going on during that time, I'm just . . . done. Evil and cruelty can become shockingly tiresome, if the only way you know how to fight back is to go numb to them.

Hannah did not want this to be a big deal. She just wanted it to go away, and had already identified the obvious and simple solution of having the streamer be managed by someone else on the team. Will could have just trusted that she was asking for a good reason, said "okay," and resolved the problem in five minutes. Instead he maneuvered through an asteroid field of potential fuck-ups, hitting most of the asteroids along the way.

At one point, while attempting to get the streamer on the line to talk about the situation, Will mistakenly sent him a message intended for Hannah. The streamer saw this message, understood that it was obviously intended for Hannah, and felt like she and Will were machinating together behind his back. He jumped to the conclusion that Hannah was using Will to fight back against the way he had been abusing her, and went to war.

It was comically and disgustingly easy for him to manipulate the people around him in this situation. He told Will that he

---

51   This was a long-distance relationship between two people who were—
      leaving the negative stuff aside for a moment—acting consensually on
      attraction to each other. Nobody in the world should be reading those
      chat logs except the two of them.

could provide chat logs which might get Hannah fired, and that threat terrified Hannah. One of his patterns of manipulation had been to threaten to share chat logs of her telling him to fuck off when he was being awful to her, as though it was inappropriate for her to be vulgar and dismissive toward a person who was openly and miserably attempting to manipulate her, but Hannah had so little faith in the men around her that threats like that had genuine power over her.

He blackmailed Will, who had bought a sous vide for Hannah for Christmas despite only just starting to work with her and not buying any other employees a Christmas gift. Will was perhaps not an impartial judge qualified to be passing verdicts on appropriate work relationships.

He even blackmailed John a little, maybe unintentionally, by mentioning that it wasn't uncommon for people to have relationships and mentioning that he knew John had been involved with one of the streamers. John freaked out and mentioned to Oliver that someone must have leaked that information. Oliver eventually blamed the leak on Hannah—one of the women John had attempted to be involved with—and added a note to her permanent HR record that she had leaked "sensitive company information."

Now Hannah felt threatened not only by her ex, but also by her bosses; she feared losing her job. She didn't hand over all of their chatlogs, but she provided a few examples from her chats with her ex and tried to defuse the situation by saying that, like in many relationships, it was just innocent conversation which eventually turned into both of them realizing that they liked each other, and that it had felt normal, at least to her. All she wanted was for him to be assigned to a different talent manager. At this point, the streamer worked out that she wasn't deliberately gunning for him and changed tack to try to save both of their jobs. He asked her to trust him.

About a month later, Oliver held a meeting where he brought in an HR firm[52] and upper management and, ignoring anything Hannah had said she wanted, discussed whether or not they should fire the streamer and make an example of him for workplace harassment of Hannah. Oliver and Will were firmly of the opinion that they should—F2K was, after all, an organization which valued women.[53] John, perhaps with a little blackmail hovering over his head, was a professional voice of reason, pointing out that nothing in the streamer's contract made having a bad relationship with someone at F2K grounds for termination, and that he had conducted himself appropriately at all other times. I don't believe he managed to mention that firing him wasn't what Hannah wanted.

On a morning that breached the point of incredulity, Hannah and the streamer teamed up to point out that neither of them wanted this to be a big deal. Neither had meant for the other to be put in such an awkward situation, and all they wanted was for the streamer to be transferred to another talent manager. They both said that this would be fine and that they didn't imagine their relationship being problematic in the future. Upper management eventually decided this was reasonable. Afterward, the streamer would leverage this example of the two of them having each other's backs to get back into Hannah's life again and continued to bring up how well they worked together for months. He expected her to overlook everything else he had done and continue her relationship with him, supported by this one incident and surrounded by the toxic waste of everything else. On top of this, they had some money issues to settle, and

---

52 An external firm hired for $10,000, because F2K's staff budget had room for Oliver's $100K+ salary but no HR department.

53 As I write this, saliva starts to well up in my mouth, preparing me to vomit like when I'm watching popping videos.

he told her they could work them out by having her arrange promotions for him on the side.[54]

Once the dust had settled, Hannah requested a couple of weeks off. She had gone straight back to work after a surgery six months earlier and still hadn't had time to heal properly.[55] This fiasco had been the final straw; she needed a break. She also mentioned she'd like to consider coming back part-time instead of full-time afterwards. Oliver told her he'd get back to her the next day. So she started chatting with a few of the people she'd been working with over the last four years to prepare them for covering her absence.

A week later,[56] Oliver got on a call with Hannah and Aleks, one of the people she'd been explaining her responsibilities to. He began by accusing her of backchanneling for talking with Aleks over the past week. Under his supervision, he allowed her and Aleks to continue to chat about when it would make sense for her to take time off, and they agreed on a date two weeks in the future, thinking it'd take that long to get things worked out and for her to finish up her current projects.

Oliver stepped in to tell her that, if she came back part-time, her compensation would be—where did I put my notes—$1,000 per month for eighty hours of work, scheduled in whatever way she saw fit. He humiliated her with this offer while Aleks was on the call, listening to the negotiation. She was stunned. She had worked at the company for four years, tackled all sorts of

---

54 This sounds a lot like indentured servitude to me, which I believe is generally frowned upon.

55 I suppose it says a lot about how miserable Hannah's treatment was in these events that, up until now, I'd found it unnecessary to mention that she was diagnosed with and beat cancer in 2020. But yeah, in a book largely about her experiences of injustice, the other injustices are repulsive enough that cancer only earns a footnote.

56 Astute readers will note that a week is significantly longer than a day.

responsibilities and challenges to grow it into a team capable of raising millions of dollars in investment capital, and she was being told that her pay would be reduced by 80% if she wanted to cut her hours back by half. A thousand dollars per month was what she'd been making five years ago when she almost single-handedly oversaw the growth of a gigantic tournament platform for one of the most important competitive games of all time, and she had been massively underpaid *then*. To add insult to injury, Oliver added that the new part-time schedule would no longer qualify her to be called F2K's "Strategic Partnerships Operations Manager," an obnoxious title he had given to the woman who was once the company's Chief of Operations. She'd never wanted it to begin with.

It's always jarring to me how much respect and appreciation Hannah has toward me just for treating her like a human being, but at the same time I can logically understand why and where it comes from.

That call happened on a Friday, and afterward she spent the weekend processing the disrespect and pain she had just endured. Not altogether an abnormal weekend for someone employed in this space.[57] I let her know that I had her back and that, if she needed help making ends meet, I could find more work for her to do for me. On Monday, she asked Aleks if he understood why she'd felt upset and disrespected by that offer, and he said "yes." He told her he had gone to Oliver afterwards on Friday and predicted that Hannah would walk.

"What did Oliver say?" she asked Aleks.

"He said he didn't care."

She quit, effective immediately, and told Aleks he could relay this to Oliver. I was still intact enough to be able to get a kick of schadenfreude out of watching the chaos unfold as the rest of

---

57 "Ladies and gentlemen, the weekend!"

the staff tried to pick up the threads of the many projects and friendships that she'd been managing at the team, and Hannah was already charging up with power from her kuyashii.

An impersonal announcement that she was no longer with the team, as though she had simply disappeared, was posted in the team Discord's official announcement channel. Streamers didn't have account privileges to post messages in the announcement channel, but could add emojis as reactions to the messages. A friend of mine reacted with a single crying cat emoji, and I added my own. The announcement was later deleted. At this point in my relationship with F2K, I started seriously imagining how my experience there might look in book or TV series form, but never imagined that I could ever feel justified in betraying the trust of people I'd worked with for years in order to actually publish something.

It's hard to write this now, knowing what is about to come next—and knowing that so many of the hints had already been dropped, and I'd ignored them.

***

Hannah re-signed with the team a couple of months later. After some discussion with me and other friends, she decided she was willing to come back as a part-time consultant through her own company so that she didn't technically answer to anyone. They had her managing the accounts and nothing else. John explained to me in a private call that they just wanted her on the team, because for some reason they'd noticed since she left that she must have been doing something that made all the streamers happy. I began to try to explain but realized he wasn't going to listen. The announcement that she had returned to the team was made on May 17, 2021, and the reactions it received were:

22 :PepoParty:'s, a meme frog with a party hat on.

9 :F2KPink:'s, the team's logo.

8 :blobDance:'s, a yellow blob shaking it.

7 :yay:'s, an anime girl with a huge smile and her hands up.

7 :zabracLove:'s, a girl with big red hearts over her eyes.

7 :COGGERS:, the meme frog again, but shaped like a cog and looking excited.[58]

6 :catparty:'s, a cat partying.

6 :pepeLove:'s, the meme frog holding a heart

4 :tajsH:'s, the same meme frog holding a slightly different heart.

3 :slysssLove:'s, a streamer who wasn't even on the team anymore making a heart with her hands and smiling.

3 :dekksH:'s, an anime boy holding a huge red heart in his hands.

1 :avngrUwu:, an anime boy blushing and looking shy. Maybe not the best choice given the behind-the-scenes context of the situation but probably meant from a good place.

No other message in the announcements thread had gotten this many reactions in the last year. The message with the second most reactions was, hilariously, an announcement which ended with "Please acknowledge that you've read this and we're on the same page with any emote," which had gotten a little over half as many. The third was one where we could enter a competition to win $250 by responding with an emote.

Hannah didn't quite get a full "O Captain! My Captain!" when she left, but she sure did when she came back.

---

58   I have no idea.

THE BETRAYAL

Oliver never got the company under control as its CEO, and the fiasco with Hannah, alongside mounting costs and little revenue, felt like the beginning of the end. A few weeks later, he forced the issue. When Rally had set up coins for streamers, they had seeded the coins with investments from Rally and F2K, which meant that Rally and F2K now owned significant amounts of their streamers' cryptocurrencies. Now, confronted with a struggling budget and mounting operational costs, he made the call to liquidate them.

The streamers were understandably furious. They had been told that their cryptocurrencies were the real deal, and they had invested tremendous amounts of work into them, running tournaments using Rally Coins as the prize pool and explaining and advertising them to their communities for the last year. Then, the organizations which originally backed them decided to cash out on their labor without consulting or warning them, and the value of their coins dropped 50% or more in one day. Not only were the streamers suddenly out a huge amount of money, but so were all of their viewers, whom they'd assured that this would be a trustworthy investment.

Now, I wouldn't ever argue that cryptocurrency *wasn't* a pyramid scheme. There are a few clear ways in which it can have real value, but it's certainly susceptible to pump-and-dump manipulation like this. Back when Oliver had pitched Rally Coin to me and I couldn't work out what its business model was, it was, I guess, because the business model was this. It's actually a pretty beautiful business model. It's arguably not even a pump-

and-dump: You sign a person with a public-facing presence, have them do a bunch of labor to make demand for a cryptocurrency for you, and then sell it. The other person's labor almost makes it legitimate, as long as you're not willing to examine anything very critically. It is beautiful in the way that a spider eating its mate is beautiful. Terribly, terribly beautiful.

F2K was in a somewhat unique position as an older team that had started in a weird jurisdiction and had a history of financial trouble. Several times, it had relied on investments from streamers, or streamers' forgoing pay in favor of equity in the company, in order to stay operational. So not only were the streamers pissed, but several of those streamers who were pissed had equity in the company and knew everyone who worked on the backend.

I talked with John quite a lot during this time. Despite the ways I've described him so far, I was still clinging to the belief that we were friends and that he was, at his core, a good person. He wasn't talking to streamers much at all, spending his days trying to solicit investments from a variety of interesting characters. At some point, he mentioned to me that he'd been chatting with one of the founders of *Magic: The Gathering* and asked if I'd be interested in doing a pack-opening of an Alpha Starter Deck (generally valued at $50,000 or more) on stream for charity. I reminded him that I thought pack-opening was awful but conceded that yes, I could be ethically pliable in certain extreme situations, and this was one of them. Somehow, the opportunity evaporated into the wind. I wondered exactly what those calls were contributing to the success of the company.

I also heard a *lot* of venting from John about Oliver. On at least one call during the Hannah and HR situation, he used D-Day-type language to describe what was about to happen between him and Oliver the next day, but so far his anger and frustration had been placated and deflected. A large part of my loss of interest in F2K stemmed from listening to John vent about how badly everything was going, which made his later betrayal of me taste even worse.

Eventually all the pressure added up, and John went to talk to Cody again. After some convincing, Cody gave John his backing to fire Oliver and take back the reins as sole CEO. The bloodbath occurred the next day; John called it a coup. Suddenly he was back in sole control of the company.

In the same way that my first call with John had been multifaceted—a fun conversation we both wanted to have which was also about joining the team—all of our others were, too. A common pattern would be that John needed someone to vent to, so he turned to me, and I was interested in hearing about things that were going on with F2K, so I was willing to listen. Strategy gamers are excellent at giving you a little of what you want in order to get what they want back from you, and when they are also socially competent, they can be powerful manipulators.

On May 31, 2021, in the second-to-last conversation I ever had with John, I told him he wasn't a jerk. In a dispute with someone over basketball cards, the other person had called him a jerk, and I told him that this guy must be wrong because I knew he wasn't a jerk. I am all about listening to friends' problems and providing words of affirmation.

A week later, Hannah let me know that she was doing payroll for the first time since coming back as a contractor, and F2K was telling her not to pay me.

I checked my bank account and realized I hadn't received a payment since March 2021—three months earlier—and asked Hannah what was going on. There was a hold on my account, and she had been given no explanation. I asked John what was happening, and he told me that Will must have done something to my account before he got fired, and that they must have missed it. He claimed that my salary was logged as $0, but nobody had noticed. I double-checked this with Hannah—again, she was contracted by F2K to keep their accounts—and she told me this didn't make any sense. The only person who would be withholding anyone's pay was John.

Just like that, my multi-year relationship with the team was reduced to a couple of cells in a spreadsheet that read "Hold for now" and "No pymt this month."

***

One of the most brutal things about the way that we abuse each other is that the mechanisms which hurt us are real. A common lie that we tell is that they are fake. That an abusive partner's love isn't real love, that a job doesn't surround you with real friends in a family-type environment, that a friend who tricks you wasn't a friend at all. But none of these things are really true. An abusive partner really does love you—it's just that their version of love is warped and hurtful. It connects to your version of love and appeals and deceives you because it is, at its core, true, even while everything that surrounds it warps it into something evil.

The "lie" about a workplace being a family environment is true, too. "We're all a family here!" is an insidious claim made by management to excuse mistreatment and underpayment of workers, and to persuade people to give their all. But when it's done well, it *is* true. They are deliberately creating an environment which pulls at the core ideas you have about how you should treat the other people on your team—your family—so that you pitch in instead of demanding appropriate pay. You might go to a boss and demand a pay raise, but if that person is framed as a father figure, you might be sated with advice or kindness instead.

And the lie about John being my friend wasn't a lie. He was my friend. When, a couple of days after this moment, he told me he might go to jail for fraud, I told him that I would come visit, and I would have, because that's what you do for a friend. He's just also a fucked-up human being.

I don't know when it happened—maybe it was always how he worked—but he learned to use the mechanisms of friendship as a way to cheat and lie to people and get what he wanted, and as working for F2K became more and more taxing, he had to lean on that behavior more and more. Maybe this isn't as vindictive and cathartic as it would be to say that he is solely awful, but if anything, I think it is scarier. I think a lot of people who are put in his position start doing awful things. I think the system they are working in makes them do this. I have searched for goliaths who stand firm against the waves of this world for the last five years, and I've only found a handful.

I told John that my not getting paid didn't make sense, and he said he knew it wasn't right and asked me how he should make it right. I told him that, for starters, the money would be good. I also suggested raising the salary cap in my contract that said I couldn't be paid more than $5,000 a month for passive advertising. When I'd signed with F2K initially, I had only been making around $1,000 a month through them, but my channel had grown significantly over the last couple of years; now I was hitting the cap or getting close to it fairly often.

We got on a call the next morning. I was twenty-four hours into the side effects of my second coronavirus vaccine shot and had slept for fourteen of them. I was nursing a bit of a headache.

He told me a few different stories. A central one that I hadn't expected was that F2K was about to go out of business and couldn't afford to pay me. He told me that he'd been incredibly depressed for the last two weeks. He told me F2K owed $200,000 to investors and that if he ever set foot in the United States again, he would be put in jail. He told me the investors were threatening to sue him. He told me he'd accidentally committed fraud on account of a new accountant keeping the books differently after

Hannah left the company, which had led him to unintentionally misrepresent F2K's financials to investors. Along with this variety of lies, half-truths, and irrelevancies, he also told me that I didn't "deserve" the money because I hadn't been running enough sponsorships for the team.

It is true that I hadn't been running as many sponsorships for the team as I could have. Although, again, my contract gave me absolute right of refusal for any sponsorship they brought me, and the sponsorships they had been bringing in the last year and a half had not been very good. I'd even reluctantly held my nose through some of the Softgiving debacle.

I reiterated that I would still like to be paid. I had continued advertising F2K on my channel, run a couple of team sponsorships that I hadn't otherwise been paid for, and fulfilled my administrative backend obligations. In the three months when I hadn't been paid, my channels, which always showed the F2K carousel—a rotating banner ad on my stream displaying the sponsors du jour—had racked up around three million new views and two and half million hours of new watch time.[59] I'd even done a bunch of extra unpaid work with Will, and had been available for calls with John whenever he'd wanted, and while I didn't expect to be paid for that, the idea that I wasn't contributing to the team was bogus. I didn't care if F2K was $200,000 in debt to other people;[60] they owed me $10,000 and had been contractually obligated to pay me for the last three

---

59 John always liked to say that this didn't mean anything because the sponsors weren't paying F2K for this, as if there were some universe where embedding advertising directly into my stream video 100% of the time that my stream was live just wasn't worth any money. If that were true, maybe they shouldn't have included it in the contract I signed as one of the responsibilities they would be paying me for.

60 I still don't even understand how this could have been true. Investors know that their investments might not pay out, but contractors receive contractual commitments that they will be paid for their work.

months. He was effectively stealing from me, directly in front of me, while telling me that he was doing it.

He told me that he'd love for me to sue him because the second someone sued F2K, the entire company would crash and he'd get to stop trying to hold it all together. That part appealed to me as possibly true.

I felt like I was losing my mind. I called one of my childhood best friends, someone with an outside perspective on what was happening, and I got about one and a half sentences into my explanation of what was happening before he said, "Yup, that's illegal."

I circled back up with Hannah, and we tried to work out what was going on.

My best guess for how this had happened is this: Back at the beginning of the year, I had been talking to John a lot about Oliver and Will, trying to communicate what was going on and why their approach wasn't working. He was "busy" talking to investors twelve hours a day and was mostly detached from day-to-day stuff, so I was giving him a lot of feedback on how things were being delivered and received, and he was talking to me about the bits and pieces that he understood of what was going on.

During this time, one of the big things John wanted was to turn the company into a sort of "insurance" for streamers. Streamers would get a baseline salary based on minutes watched, and F2K would try to sell sponsorships for them. If F2K sold two or fewer in a month, the streamers would fulfill them for no extra fee—just the salary—but if they did more, they would start to get a multiplier on their salary. Streamers could opt into different categories of sponsorships which they would automatically be signed up for.

I thought this was an absolutely awful idea. I didn't know any streamers who wanted this and was certain that I didn't. I wanted the ability to negotiate exactly the types of sponsorships I wanted to do and get paid more for them—that was my goal in being a part of F2K. I didn't want to be mandated to do sponsorships based on their category *and* be paid less.

I had explained to John that, between my distaste for this plan and my disaffection with Oliver and Will, I was losing interest in going above and beyond for the team. I wasn't going to opt into a ton of sponsorship categories. I was going to fulfill contractual obligations, and that was mostly it.

My guess is that John interpreted that as me checking out of F2K and decided to stop paying me. I would guess that he knew it was illegal; he just figured I wouldn't do anything about it. And also, it seemed like he was genuinely having some sort of depressive break. I knew he had struggled with depression in the past. For years, Hannah and the other staff members had been covering for him whenever he found himself unable to work. Often his coping method had been to check out and go play *FIFA* or another game for a few weeks until he was ready to come back.

***

Hannah has a block in her brain that prevents her from believing that the people she works with are bad people. Rather than believe her instincts that they do not appreciate her or care for her, she defaults to thinking she's dumb. She'd rather just believe that her brain is wrong. I'm a lot like her in that way, too.

But she isn't okay with people treating me poorly, and she isn't willing to believe that I'm dumb. When we talked about my conversation with John, she started talking a bit like one of the androids from *Westworld* being confronted by evidence that she was a robot. Her voice went neutral, and she said things like that it didn't "sit right" with her. At some point, she might have said something as forceful as "That isn't okay." I felt like I was pushing against a barrier in her mind which she'd put up to protect herself from trauma, and wondered if I should just drop it. She found herself in an awful position where she needed to stand up for me—something she loved to do more than almost anything, far more than standing up for herself—but this time, that meant confronting John.

***

Having a following of a hundred thousand people is a powerful thing. If I need art made, I say so, and someone incredible puts their hand up to say I can commission them. Once when I needed voice work done for a project, I got an email from Ray Chase, a professional voice actor who wanted to do it for free. He later came on the channel for a charity event and read a bunch of our favorite chat messages from the history of the channel in tons of hilarious different voices. When I was taking a break from my regular games to play some chess, Peter Svidler came on—straight out of the annals of my bible, *500 Grandmaster Games of Chess*—to beat me repeatedly for the amusement of my viewers. At the start of the coronavirus pandemic, some researchers asked if they could join me to explain how they were using computers to build prototype interventions against it, and together we showed off a gamified program where you could sit down and fold proteins to try to build something which would float around in someone's body and bind with COVID-19's binders to neutralize them. When I travel, it's not unheard of for the head of a gaming company to reach out and ask if I would like a tour.

I quickly discovered that I could find lawyers in the same way. By the end of the day, private conversations with a couple of viewers had connected me directly to a full-time esports lawyer.

But I never needed the lawyer; I still had Hannah. She set up a call with John for the next morning. The first thing he said to her was "jorbs is never going to see a cent of that money," but by the end of the call, F2K had made plans to pay me the full balance in installments over the next four months. In the end, perhaps unsurprisingly, I didn't get all the money, but I did receive the first installment the next day, and it was better than nothing. I thought about how much I'd be willing to spend to sue them anyway. I had a huge moment of emotional catharsis—the end of my time with F2K, coupled with my second vaccine giving me a moment of feeling safe from the coronavirus—and sat down to write my feelings. After two days, I had 15,000 words, and I looked up how long a book was, and decided, "why not?" A book would be a much better use of my time than a lawsuit, and would help me with a lot of other things, too.

***

One of the successful tricks I've found in content creation is to provide layers of depth. A new viewer comes to the channel, and I say "hi." That's an amount of attention that I can give them live. They watch for a while and see that I'm doing something differently from what they'd expect, so they ask if I can explain, but I've already given them the amount of attention that I have available for them, so instead I send them to a YouTube video where I spend ten minutes answering the question fully. They come back and say, "Wow, that's cool! Do you have a video which talks a bit more about your general strategy for things like this?" and I send them to a four-hour long video where I outline my structural thought processes for playing the game and solving situational problems in it. They're sold and subscribe to the channel to keep watching my content; maybe they even head down the YouTube content rabbit hole and watch more of my videos there.

I have that set up well for games, but not for my personality. I've made a video that's targeted at other aspiring content creators which talks about the things I think are important in growing a channel, building a community, and establishing yourself once you have, but I've never worked out how to make a video that tells a viewer who doesn't know me about the things which are important to me. It doesn't feel like something which fits properly into a video. They'll work it out over time by hanging out in my community, but that's a lot of time to spend in a world where people want all of it at once. So, here's a book instead. Thanks, John. I guess.

***

Over the next few weeks, I chatted with many of my friends from the team. Some had left a while ago—many had lost faith when they were asked to work without pay, or weren't okay with the Softgiving strong-arm. Some had been hanging on begrudgingly, honoring their end of their contract but nothing more, enjoying the extra pay. Some had so much invested in the team that they didn't feel like they could get away; for a few, it didn't matter if the team treated them badly when it was backing their cryptocurrency, which might be worth a million dollars. (F2K had started liquidating their own holdings in streamers' Rally Coins, but held onto enough to keep control of them.) In one case, I was told by a streamer that F2K had made more money from their Rally Coin than the full amount they had actually paid the streamer over years on the team. They still managed to go bankrupt.

I soon started hearing that they were all getting calls from John. He was saying that the team was imploding and that they shouldn't expect their contracts to continue. Hannah took the work she'd been doing to find sponsorships for me and used it as evidence that she could help other streamers if they'd like. Not only did she end up with a couple of other streamers as clients, but two of her friends—those rare guys at F2K who had treated her like a human—were willing to jump ship to work for her at her own new company. When I told her she'd be making more than me soon, she thought it was a joke, but I showed her how I could fairly easily see that being true with a year or so of work.

In the end, she found something completely different.

CONTROL

There are many ways to control a person. Some are benevolent: You can be a leader. Some types of control are consensual and desired. Others are not. When I learned to beat others at poker, I didn't just learn how to play my cards right; I learned how to read which cards they were most likely to have and how to manipulate the way they would play their own cards so that it favored me. How to make them call if they had a hand worse than mine, or fold if they had one better than me. How to let them bluff into me when I was strong and they were weak. At my worst, I learned which of the regulars I'd played a lot of hands with was in a bad mood that night, and tried to position myself to profit from their frustration. And I learned which of the newer players at the online tables were drinking, and tried to ingratiate myself to them so that they'd keep playing with me. The avatar I used was a picture of Jessica Alba in a bright blue dress with a huge smile. It was my second choice; the first had been rejected for being too sexual. My username was a string of random numbers so that my opponents were less likely to think of me as a human. It can seem harder to manipulate a machine.

I stopped playing poker because I was exhausted and disgusted by who it was empowering me to be, but I never stopped wanting control. The little gremlin sitting at the controls in my head wants to understand all of the resources available to me, how they connect, and how to maneuver them.

It's not an abstractly evil desire to have. Painters look at a palette and understand how to make their canvas sing. Conductors stand in front of an orchestra and understand how to make it fill the concert hall. I've tried to build a comfortable community where I play zero-stakes games and explain the ways I exert control over those games so that others can relax and learn from me. Sometimes it can feel dangerous, though. It's a desire which tends to consume everything around you, if you let it.

I am playing a couple of games in my free time right now. Now that I stream for a living, I don't like spending as much of my recreational time on gaming as I used to, but I'll still sit down and vibe with a game for an hour or two every now and then. My favorite is called *Celeste*, a platformer in which you control a pixelated character who is trying to jump and climb her way up a mountain. *Celeste* is, ultimately, a game about control.

The most obvious exertion of control in *Celeste* is that of myself on the character. I move her. I push my controller's analog stick to the right, and she moves right. I push it to the left, and she moves left. As I play through the game, it teaches me more and more ways to manipulate that movement. I can jump; I can grab hold of things. I can combine jumping and grabbing hold of things in a variety of ways. I can dash; I can double-dash. By combining buttons, I can hyperdash, or extended hyperdash, or wavedash. My jumps can carry momentum, or slide along walls. I can make the character fall faster, a very simple technique which I'm never forced to implement until a screen very late in the game, and which I consequently realize I should have been doing the entire time to increase my speed, making me go back and re-learn the patterns for many previous solutions. I can perform demodashes through obstacles as long as there is a gap of three pixels in their hitboxes, using an unintended and very precise combination of button inputs which were discovered by people trying to speedrun the game, and which the game's developer embraced and added more support for after it was discovered.

The first time I see a level, I look at it and hypothesize which combination of controls might successfully take me through it.

The hundredth time I see that level, I recognize that there's been a slightly faster way to beat it this entire time, but it will require me to perform two dashes which are quite difficult and time a jump precisely to preserve momentum from a moving platform. As I play, I become a master of controlling this character, in the same way that I can master control of a piano or guitar through hours of practice. The game invites me into my element and allows me to explore it.

The second most obvious element of control in *Celeste* is its story. The game is about a girl who goes to climb a mountain because she is overcome with self-doubt and wants to prove that she can succeed. But the only way she can succeed is, ironically, by accepting her doubt as part of herself, and using it to strengthen her abilities. It is a story of self-acceptance, which is one of the most powerful and important types of control we can exert in our lives. The game's creator came out as trans shortly after releasing it, and that context has brought particular life to the story's subtext and made it a centering point for trans identities in online gaming.

But it's the third type of control that I want to examine when talking about *Celeste*: it lets me control the context in which I play the game. When I bought *Celeste*, several years ago, I paid $19.99 for it in an online game store. The game's creator got most of that money, with the online store taking a (mostly) fair cut. Since then, I have played the game for 310 hours and have never been asked to pay another dollar for it. When a major expansion to the game was released, adding a new level with several new mechanics and musical scores, it was simply added to my game for no further charge, for me to enjoy whenever I wanted to download and play it.

While I play *Celeste*, I am in control of my choice to play the game. The story guides me, and the levels set my challenges, and I sit at my computer and become a master of this mountain, without having to worry about my pursuit of control hurting the people around me; the game refuses to consume any part of me other than the time I give it. Because of this, I have spent a paltry six cents for every hour of enjoyment I've gotten from it. But on the other hand: It has become my favorite game; I will remember it and talk about it until I die; I have spent approximately 750 words telling readers how incredible it is in this book I am publishing. For a competitive marketing strategy, this is not the worst outcome possible.

I will not be naming the other game I am playing right now, because I do not want you to try it. It is a game built for mobile phones which I ran a sponsored segment for on my channel, and then continued to play after that stream. I wouldn't usually have played it at all, let alone as a sponsored segment, but in the wake of the U.S. Supreme Court's decision to overturn *Roe v. Wade*, I decided that I wanted to take some extra sponsorships I would usually turn down and then donate the money to abortion funds, so here we are.

In this new game, I assemble a team of fighters who are then pitted against other players' teams of fighters. In each battle, one team wins; the other loses. Bright lights flash as slick animations play during the battles, but the players themselves have little input. I am told what team I will play against ahead of time (my opponent isn't even present in real time), and I can take as long as I would like to rearrange my pieces, or substitute in new ones to counter theirs. Then I press "battle" and sit and watch what happens.

Conceptually, this game seems like it is also about putting me in control. I learn what all the different fighters do, and which enemy fighters they can counter. The central refrain is simple and genuinely enjoyable; I'm still playing because I'm finding it fun.

The problem though, is the context, because the context of this game is not about empowering me to be in control. The

223

game is "free to play," which means that anyone can download it and start playing it for free. But the second that you download the game, it starts trying to manipulate you to pay money.

Do you like this fighter and want to level him up? Here's a pack which will contain experience for him for $1.99. Oh, that wasn't enough? Here's one for $5.99 with more experience per dollar spent. These packs go up to $99.99 super-packs, and buying one of those won't even give you 5% of the experience required to fully max out your fighters for the game.

In theory, of course, it is free to play, and you can level up your fighters over time. But if you really want to do that, you should buy the monthly pass, which will give you more rewards for completing daily quests and allow you to increase the speed of battles so that you can earn more experience per hour.

And the daily quests. Oh, my. The powers in charge of this game clearly took note when grocery stores worked out that giving customers chances to buy guilty treats would prey on their inability to say "no" over and over again, and then amped the concept up by a thousand. I am rewarded with a chest for playing for five minutes every six hours, and in order to open it I have to enter the game's store, where I am shown the current "best deals." I have daily quests, weekly quests, daily challenges, a plethora of game modes which exist primarily as a means of giving me opportunities to spend money on microtransactions. If I ever do play for more than thirty minutes at once I quickly find that I've finished all my quests for the day and there just . . . isn't anything left to do? Which I suspect is deliberate; the game isn't intended to be fun to play for a long time, it's intended to inject itself into your thoughts throughout the day, to make you think "oh, I could just log in and do a few battles now to open my chest" and then find yourself exposed to another opportunity to upgrade your majestic himbos for the low price of $99.99.

While I love playing *Celeste*, my experience of the online world—both as a consumer on Twitter, Twitch, and YouTube, and as a contractor working on those platforms and with businesses surrounding those platforms—is much more resonant with my time spent watching my himbos do battle in their online arena. F2K's story was one of control. Certainly at a smaller scale than that of Amazon's, but perhaps not at a less powerful intensity for those caught up in it. [61]

For almost half of my life at this point, I've been controlled by gaming in a third type of way, one that is even more challenging to combat. I have been dependent on it for my income. Socially, we understand that adults must earn money to pay for food and rent, and as such it is normal for many people to be dependent on employers for jobs.[62]

As a gamer, I've been put in a variety of complex and unique situations because of this dependence. While I played poker, my ethical concerns were occasionally subordinate to my need to pay rent, and I felt similarly when I was starting out as a streamer. When I finally reached the point where I was comfortably making enough money to make ends meet, I took a step back and realized that I was dissatisfied with many of the ways I had chosen to run my channel, and spent a couple of years moving away from some habits I disliked which had helped me monetize it, like soliciting donations or promoting products I didn't actually feel my viewers would be well served by purchasing.

But, for the most part, this has never been a major difficulty for me, because I have been *successful* as a gamer and content creator. The pressure of dependence on employment doesn't feel

---

61   And with F2K I got to see something quite breathtaking: I got to see what happened when that control was threatened, and then fell apart.

62   I would argue that this is an awful injustice, but it is undeniably the way the world currently works.

as heavy when you have $60,000 in your savings account, or three thousand people watching you and supporting you. The same has not been true for all of my friends.

For example, when I had a viewer donate enormous amounts of money to my channel, requesting increasingly uncomfortable (and sometimes sexually charged) favors from me as reciprocation, I set a strong boundary—and when he crossed it, I banned him from my channel. Some of my friends, placed in similar situations, have had to choose to keep entertaining viewers like him, because otherwise they wouldn't be able to pay their rent.

Throughout Hannah's career, this had been her lot. At F2K she struggled to stand up to John, or Benji, or Oliver, because she feared losing her job. She quit the company multiple times but kept coming back, partially because of how much she loved looking after the streamers, but also because she needed the money, even though she could tell that it was an unhealthy work environment for her.

After she left F2K, I finally got to see her succeed.

Ironically, I found out about Hannah's success from her abusive streamer ex, who was still trying to control her. They had been trying to be friends again, and he had found out that she was getting involved in a play-to-earn cryptocurrency game, and he had freaked out and told her that it was a pyramid scheme. Perhaps that was somewhat true, but my opinion is that he just didn't like her being around other people. He had convinced her to quit playing *World of Warcraft* with her friends, and once told her that I was grooming her and manipulating her by using money to get her to do what I wanted. ("That's called a job," she had laughed at him.)

After she'd responded to him freaking out by blocking him everywhere for the umpteenth time, he messaged me about it.[63] This was the first time I'd talked with him at any length since he and Hannah had first dated, but we'd never officially argued about anything or blocked each other, and we were still technically colleagues. I chose to talk to him for a bit, although in retrospect I feel like it was a mistake, and that Hannah would have preferred to have me ignore his messages.

It was anxiety inducing and frightening to participate in a conversation with him, knowing what had been going on between him and Hannah. He asked if we could voice chat, and I lied and said that I couldn't get to a microphone, wanting to have a text record of everything we said. He started by prying for information—he wanted to "clear the air" and wanted to know why I'd "ghosted" him. When I told him I felt it would be professionally and personally wrong for me to be friendly with him because of the awful relationship he'd had with my employee and friend, he insisted that it was unfair that I wasn't being his friend anymore.

As the conversation went on, he pried for information and then warped it in order to manipulate me. It was like he was trying to work out what reasonable goals he could achieve as the conversation continued, changing what he was trying to get from me based on what I said. Eventually he gave up on trying to convince me that he and Hannah were fine together[64] and moved on to telling me that she was investing in a pyramid

---

63 As of writing this draft, Hannah still hasn't found any way to stop him from coming after her. If she blocks his email, he makes a new account. If she blocks his number, he makes a new one and won't stop calling her phone until she picks up. He watches my Twitch channel to see what I'm doing and hear me talk about her. He has threatened to come to her house. More than once, he has messaged her friends to get to her; this time, he messaged me.

64 They weren't even dating at the time, so I'm genuinely not sure what he thought he meant. He was messaging me about her because she'd blocked him on every messaging app he had her contact information on.

scheme and that I should be worried about it. I told him she was an adult, and she could do what she wanted, and it wasn't my job to worry about her, which I felt was somewhat transparently not a statement about myself but rather a comment on his own behavior—me manipulating him back.

Yeah, I play strategy games too. Throughout my life, I've sat on his side of these conversations and felt evil parts of my brain insist that I manipulate and scheme my way through them, but hey, look at me: I've learned better ways to interact with people. I grew up.

When I talked with Hannah about the conversation, later, I told her that I'd been blown away by how powerfully manipulative he was. Even knowing what was happening, I still felt worried when he claimed she was investing in a pyramid scheme. He had some part of me under his spell.

For me, it all broke apart when he insulted me. When I insisted that it wasn't my place to tell Hannah what to do, he said, "I wouldn't know what it's like to be so apathetic about everything, I guess," and the entire illusion shattered. If this had been targeted at someone who had been broken down for years—to the point where she saw having self-published a serial novel that her middle school classmates enjoyed reading as evidence that she was dumb because the writing hadn't been perfect—an insult like that might land and manipulate its victim into thinking he was the one who knew what was going on, and she should trust him more than she trusted herself. For me . . . no. I let others put me down in my early twenties, but I don't fuck with that anymore. I'm manipulable, but you have to do it in other ways.[65]

I did check in with her about what was going on. This was the first time he'd come to me to talk about their relationship, and it

---

65 Historically, the best way to manipulate me is to tell me you care about me and then ask me nicely to do something.

was a new sort of breach of trust and conduct. She was furious at him. She explained that she had blocked him everywhere that morning; he must have contacted me to try to get to her. She'd blocked him everywhere countless times for months, but he kept on slithering back through whatever crack he could, and he—and the rest of the world—had broken her down so much that eventually she couldn't keep saying no.

After she'd settled their money issues by finding sponsorship deals for him, she'd finished blocking him everywhere, and he responded by sending her $69 using the only means of communication he had left—their payment system. He is deplorable. I am an extremely non-violent person—I almost never have violent thoughts of any sort—but I once spent a fifteen-minute walk visualizing what it would be like to throw him through a window of a high floor of a skyscraper. And then I started thinking, maybe a slightly lower floor, so I'd be able to see the body more easily. I have never had a thought like that about anyone else in my life. But Hannah told me that she'd deal with it herself, and I certainly wasn't going to help the situation by being another man who ignored what she wanted, so I stepped away and let her handle it.

A few days later, he sent her an email, and she came to me for support. I walked through it with her, sentence by sentence. "This is him lying to you to try to win your sympathy." "Here he is stating a false dilemma to try to make it seem like he will flounder without your help—there are millions of ways he could solve this without needing you to do anything." "This sentence is just pathetic. He needs to grow up." "All of these problems are being manufactured to make it seem like he needs your help, and none of the ways he is appealing to your past relationship, or claiming he wants to be your friend, have anything to do with honest love or friendship."

I'm a strategy gamer. I know.

The next time he sent her an email, she went through it sentence by sentence on her own, and told me that she remembered the things I'd showed her and how I'd read it, and that it didn't have its power over her anymore. He still wouldn't leave her alone, but at least now she felt confident in her ability to see his insults and manipulations for what they were.

Hannah hadn't invested in a pyramid scheme. Well, except insofar as all cryptocurrency is a pyramid scheme, I guess. What she'd actually done was started her own business, with a hefty initial investment from her father. The business centered on the game *Axie Infinity*, a Pokémon-type game which used Non-Fungible Tokens (NFTs) on the Ethereum blockchain. Every time a new "Axie" was made, it was added to the blockchain, meaning it could be traded and owned by different players. The best Axies went for hundreds of dollars; in the Philippines, a huge culture had sprung up built around using Axies to grind the game as a job to earn real money.

Most people in the world would have no idea what was going on here—you're forgiven if what you've read so far doesn't make much sense. The few people who did understand what was going on were using it to make money for themselves. They started lending their Axies to Filipino players—who would use them to grind for in-game resources to sell for real money—in exchange for ludicrous cuts of the earnings. Eighty percent seemed like a standard rate. Some of these lenders even asked for down payments before they would let players use their Axies.

I have complex opinions about this phenomenon. My opinions about cryptocurrency are complex; my opinions about a game built on cute graphics which might appeal to children, but which can also be used by players to make money, are complex. My opinions on loaning out pieces from a game and charging 80% for their use are mostly straightforward but a little bit complex at times. One thing is not complex though, and that's what Hannah does.

I like to say that, when you're confronted by something very complicated, whether in life or in a game, it's often easier to work out what it's going to do if you can determine who has control of it and what their motivations are. You don't need to know how cryptocurrency and non-fungible tokens work to understand that a greedy person is going to use them to try to make money. And hopefully, if you've read this book, you won't be surprised to hear what Hannah did next.

She took a bunch of cash, invested it in Axies, and started loaning them out to Filipino players, taking 35% of what they earned with her Axies and putting it straight back into her community. She used skills she'd built over years of working in the online space to build an incredible community server, which immediately exploded. She made a Twitter account, which blew up. She started streaming a bit, mostly just so she could talk about what she was doing with the people who wanted to borrow Axies from her, and her stream took off.

Suddenly she had fans. It took her only two weeks to surpass where I had been two years into my streaming career. She was suddenly the figurehead of a virally exploding online community. She loaned one of her followers $1,600 at 0% interest so he could buy a good laptop to play the game and work on his university courses. When the Philippines suffered some extreme weather, she asked people in her community if they would be willing to put together aid packages and deliver them to people in need if she provided money for them to do so; suddenly, instead of finding me a good charity to raise money for, she'd essentially created her own.

The shitty men stopped weighing her down, her kuyashii ignited, and she launched.

Every dollar she made went straight back into the community she was building. No one could lie to her about who she was anymore; now she had hundreds of people telling her the truth every day. The woman who had been betrayed by her father, team, partner, even by her own body, sat down and made herself an entire new family, from scratch, and it took her two weeks.

***

I have some guilt about benefiting so much just from knowing Hannah. Over the course of our working relationship, I've tried to pay her well, and she often tries not to let me. One of the reasons is that I value the emotional labor and support that she provides me and think I should be paying for it appropriately, while she thinks that it is basically nothing and would be happy to give it to me for free. I think a tremendous amount of my success has happened because I found her. I appreciated her and empowered her to do what she was capable of, but while she gave me incredible boosts, I wasn't able to offer much more back than my respect and a paycheck, and I used her abilities in service of my own goals.

When I saw that she was achieving great things on her own now, I told her that she could stop working for me whenever she wanted. It had been great, but she was destined for bigger things. I knew I'd miss her—I had no idea how I'd find anyone who could replace her—but I was excited to know that I'd get to see her doing something she loved, shining and succeeding in this world.

And, of course, she is Hannah, so she responded by telling me that she would continue working for me as long as I would let her, and that I wouldn't ever be able to stop her from loving and helping and protecting me for the rest of my life.

"Don't be crazy," she told me.

REDISCOVERY

Over the last year or two, I have been morbidly enchanted by the online rationalist community. A friend partially responsible for introducing me to them describes my topic of fascination as "the intellectual climate of a group of people who just decided to found an episteme on blogs written by two to five truly gifted but often quite myopic dudes," and while I don't know whether that's precisely true, it sounds accurate in its messiness and absurdity.

It is a bizarre window into the struggles and thoughts of a group of incredibly intelligent and privileged people, and at first I thought I would be interested and maybe even drawn in by them. They claim—by name—to be seeking rational understanding of the world, which seems like it would be a cool thing. But often when I read the things they have to say, I feel my skin crawl.

I think the explanation is that there is no coherent rationalist and universal model for truth, or if there is, it is certainly not being found by these talented people talking with each other on social media. The problems are twofold: Firstly, there is no universal data. All of our experiences are different, meaning we should all reach different conclusions about the world. Rationalist conversations seem to discard this idea, promoting the stances they arrive at as enlightened and correct for everyone.

Take effective altruism, for example. It is, at first glance, a compelling idea. You have some money and want to use it to do good in the world, so you need to do some analysis to work out the best way to spend it. In the effective altruism community, you can find spreadsheets and blog posts and lengthy arguments about the best ways to spend this money to improve the world by doing things like buying mosquito nets in India or funding AI safety research. But as someone who has cared a lot about charity work for more than a decade, effective altruism makes me want to shrivel up and die. You cannot take my morality based on my interfacing with the world throughout my life and supersede it with an algorithmic approach to morality based on the experiences of others and some data someone else arranged and analyzed. It disempowers me and destroys my agency and passion. It's like telling someone who loves film that their favorite films are bad, and that the correct way to consume film is to set the YouTube algorithm to autoplay, and *those* videos are in fact the best films the world has ever made.

Which brings up the second problem: The conclusions aren't right. The method of investigation being used, an attempt to methodically and causally demonstrate connections, is insufficient for actually finding much truth in the real world, especially when it is applied by people with no actual experience with the thing they're trying to examine. It draws conversation to realms rich in data, without anywhere near enough calibration of which parts of that data are important, and when the conversation turns to other aspects of life where data is less available, the conclusions and behaviors quickly flounder.

When I read about an AI company cancelling its robotics department because they were unsuccessful in collecting enough data about the real world for the robots to succeed, I thought immediately of rationalists. They place an immense amount of faith in causal reasoning and testable hypotheses which is frankly undeserved. Causal reasoning and testable hypotheses are tools which are useful for finding truth in some regions of life when applied precisely by experts; they aren't guaranteed to tell you useful things. Even the strategy games I play are generally too complex for these tools to be very useful in them.

Take this apparatus, strap someone with some developmental trauma on top of it, give them thousands of social media followers, and tell them that it makes them enlightened, and you get some truly weird things. For example, one morning, a few weeks after I left F2K, I woke up and read a thread where a guy was recounting—basically without filter, as far as I could tell—an acid trip where he realized he resented his parents for giving him $100,000 for his birthday, along with his thoughts about what the experience of other people whose parents didn't give them $100,000 for their birthday might be and asides like "and then i was like oh my god am i a spoiled rich kid???"

Over time, I've gone from thinking that this community is actually enlightened and intelligent to thinking this community is a lot like the *Magic: The Gathering* forums I posted on as a kid, and that, as such, it provides an interesting perspective into some of the problems with strategy gaming, reflected onto a slightly different space.

In my teens, I ascended fairly rapidly through the ranks of *Magic: The Gathering Online*. It was the first place I demonstrated excellence in strategy gaming, and I met others who were similarly excellent at games. I also spoke to the Magic community socially, and that was not at all excellent. For example, I found out what the word "twink" meant when I, still a kid, posted a picture of myself visiting Washington, D.C., on a message board and a grown man there called me a twink as an insult. A lot of the policing of bad behavior in a community like this was more about logical discussion of whether the behavior was bad than about actually punishing it.

My understanding of how to interact with a woman—or even a man who didn't play games—was almost nonexistent, because my social circles were self-contained, stagnant, and full of gatekeeping and identifying ourselves as an in-group, different from everyone else. That's what I found myself reminded of, as I learned more about the rationalist community.

That isn't to say everything about the community is bad. It is full of impressive people, some of whom are clearly brilliant. These people are finding a community they enjoy, making friends, getting married to each other and having kids, reading cool books, having interesting conversations, launching interesting ideas, and so on and so on. I would be drawn to it if I'd lived a different life and missed the experiences which gave me unique and deliberate perspectives on parts of the world which differ from theirs.

But it is also insular and built on repeated mistakes and pretending to be some things which it isn't. Observing it as an outsider feels like walking into a party where everyone is dressed a certain way, saying, "Oh whoops, I didn't realize this was a themed party!"—and then having everyone look at you like they don't understand what you mean before going back to talking with the other people there about things you've never heard of. Or maybe they talk about things you have heard of, but they've already decided exactly what they think about them, and it doesn't mesh properly with your own experiences of the real world or fails to incorporate some basic social mechanic which everyone else you know uses to mitigate or acknowledge the world's problems—something like kindness or shame.

I once went to a party in the Seattle area where the host explained that he didn't like his wife compulsively apologizing for things, so he bought a Nerf gun and started shooting her with it whenever she apologized to condition her to stop apologizing. It was unclear exactly what I was meant to think when presented with something like that. I held the gun in my hands for a bit, and it was gigantic and loaded multiple darts at once. My then partner—a person who had actually studied and implemented psychology and counseling in professional situations[66]—and I had a side-conversation about how this experiment was not peer reviewed and almost certainly was not achieving its intended result, while our host's wife breast-fed their newborn child.

Acid trips and other journeys of discovery seem to be a recurring theme in this community. Many rationalists love running uncontrolled experiments on their own brains, I believe with the presumption that said brains move closer to enlightenment. And while I find so many things foreign and bizarre about the community, I have to admit that I sort of do that too; I change my brain with my *Slay the Spire* challenges.

***

It is very hard for me to diagnose problems that I have with my stream. I go to work, often for more than eight hours a day, and thousands of different people send me thousands of different messages, and I interact with many different programs and interfaces, and outside disturbances happen, and at the end of the day, I stop working and return to the rest of my life. While a viewer might naturally assume that my stream is the important part of my life because it's the one they see—I'm regularly asked if something about the stream is bad when I seem like I have low energy or feel upset—the opposite is the truth. My stream is a subsection of my life. I put a lot of emotional and mental energy into it, and it makes me money, challenges me, and provides me job satisfaction, but the rest of my life—where I chat and do things with friends and go on hikes and eat food and sleep and see my family—is the most important thing I have. If I seem upset

---

66   After being abused for two years, my next major relationship was with a trained counselor who was especially good at working with children. You're welcome to read between the lines on that one, if you'd like. I certainly have.

on stream, the most likely explanation is that I slept poorly or had something upsetting happen to me away from the broadcast.

Because my stream isn't actually *that* much of a deal to me, and because it is an incredibly complicated thing, it can be hard for me to tell what I like and dislike about it. If something frustrates me at work, and I end my day feeling irritable, I often don't really know why and don't have enough interest or time to work it out.

Sometimes it's simply that I didn't have enough energy to cater to the requests of hundreds of strangers, and so I'm empty now and have been running on fumes for the last few hours. Other times, it's something very different—maybe I have particular feelings about a sponsorship which I ran which I haven't had time to examine, or maybe it was too hot in the office and I feel physically miserable, or maybe noise from outside was bugging me all day.

Streaming isn't a job where I take time to recognize my surroundings all that often; I sometimes spend hours streaming without sound because I am too busy focusing on the game I'm playing, the viewers who are asking me questions, and so on, and don't realize I haven't put my headphones back on. Imagine the captivation you might feel when you do something you love—looking at the time and realizing four hours have passed in an instant—and then add the pressure and complexity of entertaining three thousand people while you're doing that, and you might be able to see how I might not take a moment to recognize that my chair is uncomfortable.

I'm also acting the entire time that I'm live. Over the years, I've learned to commodify certain entertaining aspects of my self, and while I stream I constantly highlight those parts of my psyche while suppressing others. I lean into my calm voice, and lengthy explanations of things, and my audience rewards me with applause and donations. At the same time, I try to suppress itches on my face, and instead of letting out stress I store it in my shoulders—or, as the stream goes on, more and more other parts of my body, until I shift slightly and double over in pain because my foot is cramping after I've sat with it fully curled and tense for the last hour. Streaming attacks the parts of my existence which my viewers don't like, and makes it harder and harder for me to engage with them. In an eight-hour show, it is normal for me to be on camera and under observation by thousands of people for the entire time other than five to ten minutes of bathroom breaks.

To diagnose and fix these problems, I set myself challenges in streaming. When I moved into a new apartment and set up my office, I wanted to find out what it was like to stream in it, so I streamed for two hundred hours in thirty days. There are some things that I can't work out just by thinking about them, and if I don't discover those things and address them, they will be constantly stressing or discomforting me every day of my life. So, I push myself and my brain toward breaking points to see what things bug me when I exhaust my capacity to simply put them aside.

Slay the Spire challenges make me realize that I need to update my glasses prescription, or force me to interact with the heat in my office and find cooling solutions for it, or give me a reason to find music I like listening to while I stream and work out how to listen to that music (which I can't legally play in a way viewers would hear) without missing stream notifications.

These challenges are also motivational. As well as diagnosing my problems, they give me a reason to fix them. If I realize I am being bugged by people asking a certain question over and over again, I suddenly feel a need to create an answer to the question I can direct them to, instead of just figuring that I'll be able to cope with it.

The comparison of streaming two hundred or more hours in a month to a drug experience doesn't hold perfectly. But, because it is fun, and sort of true, after I left F2K I started to think of my challenges as my version of a permanently brain-altering acid trip. As my relationship with F2K imploded, I started one challenge in May 2021, and then, with the dust settled, I embarked on another in July.

Much like I'd stopped putting energy into my charity streams, and instead started using them to draw energy from others, I also started to repurpose my challenges as a way to reestablish myself instead of test myself. In May, I was miserable and distracted. Everything was going wrong. F2K was imploding, and I was blown completely off course. The goal of the challenge was simple: I tried to beat *Slay the Spire*, at the highest difficulty, as many times as I could in thirty days—720 hours. I finished May with a hundred wins, which was equal to my initial goal but far fewer than I knew myself to be capable of. I took a month, wrote the first draft of this book, and then sat down in July to push myself even harder. My personal record at that point was 127, set in January, and now I intended to break it.

The challenge began with heat exhaustion. A historic heatwave had just hit the Seattle area; on the day that I intended to start, I woke up to find myself clammy, nauseous, and struggling to speak fluidly. My apartment was on the top floor of our building and got direct sunlight, and the portable air conditioning unit I had wasn't enough to cool down my office, which was hitting ninety-five degrees during the day and staying above ninety past midnight.

My then partner and I took the cats and hid in my parents' basement for a couple of days. I laid on the bed with ice packs on my feet and head for the first half day, drafting and publishing ludicrous fever-dream tweets. When I returned to the apartment, I saw that my blinds had melted.

I am working on moving as close to the South Pole as I can, but haven't gotten it all worked out yet.

There was nothing to do but play *Slay the Spire*. That is the beautiful thing. The challenge reduced my life to a simply-stated optimization problem, and I've felt at home in those since I was four. I gave the rest of my brain a break. I wasn't thinking about sexism anymore, or injustice, or a pandemic. I wasn't thinking about friendships. I was thinking about *Slay the Spire*, and I am damn good at that. In the first twenty days, I extended two of my personal best win streaks, falling one short of the Ironclad[67] World Record with eleven wins in a row, and four short of the Watcher[68] World Record with twenty. I already had World Record streaks for the other characters, so I was five wins away from holding every World Record at the same time, closer than I'd been since before the game's fourth and final character was released.

But that was not my goal—my goal was to win fast. By the morning of July 21st, with ten days left, I needed another forty-seven wins to beat my goal. I was playing as much as I could, and I was still four or five wins behind pace. It was also my father's sixtieth birthday, and I was going to take a half day to spend the afternoon with him. I decided it was time. I couldn't be thinking about world record streaks; I had to push my speed of play. My twenty-win streak on Watcher, the sum of thirty hours of constant success, ended with a run which I barely took time to think about, and I moved on from it immediately.

When I am playing *Slay the Spire* calmly, my runs clock an hour and a half or so each. This gives me time to think, interact with viewers, maybe tell a joke or go on a tangent for a bit. An ideal run, from a content perspective, is something like thirty minutes of focused play, thirty minutes of joking around, and thirty minutes of

---

67   A burly, demonic character who defeats enemies by hitting them very hard. The game's first character, usually considered its simplest.
68   A blind monk who dances between states of wrath and calm, rewarding careful play with extremely powerful output.

chatting with my audience. I play tremendously quickly compared to many other players, some of whom spend more like three or four hours on each run. Even if I'm spending time on something else, like interacting with my audience, the extra minutes in the run are still valuable. They let my brain process and internalize what's going on and improve my ability to orient myself correctly with regard to the decisions I'm making. That morning, I tried to increase my speed to bring my runs down to an hour each. I lost, a lot. It was hard. After a break to spend time with my dad, I took a nap and then continued playing, and lost even more. I lost eight runs in a row. It was the most I had lost in more than a year. After starting my day at 4:30 a.m., I went to sleep at 4:00 a.m. the next morning, having recorded two wins and twelve losses. For the first time, I was not sure if I could do this.

But I slept, and my brain recognized what I needed it to do and rewired itself and replenished. I can see it, inside my head that night, massaging the block of neurons which know about *Slay the Spire* to disconnect them from stressors and traumas which I didn't have time for anymore, connecting my eyes directly to them, and connecting them straight to my fingers. The highway system that had been gridlocked before with thoughts about whether other people approved of me, or whether I was worth anything, shut down, and I traveled on high-speed rail for combat calculations. Things I loved lined the path, shielding my thoughts from distress. Memories of how John had treated me—which had lain open on the coffee table of my mind—slammed shut and flew to the bookshelf, which became a frame to hang posters and whiteboards detailing the enemies and events in the game, covering the spines of the books I didn't need. My grandfather smiled at me. He was the morning sun, warming my face.

I woke up, and suddenly I could do it. Suddenly everything flowed. The waves were calm and I was sailing, and the people on board were happy. My sails caught the wind at the perfect angle, and its power made me strain and flex, but I held. I won, and then I won again. I won in fifty-something minutes. I won in fifty-something minutes four times in a row. In one streak, I won thirteen games out of fourteen and was one win away from extending my rotating character world record at the time. I felt possessed, but I felt clarity—I could close my eyes, and there were no demons, there were only gods.

I couldn't hold onto that feeling forever; it was too hard. Going on a streak where you win thirteen out of fourteen runs of *Slay the Spire* at max difficulty in under two days is inhuman. I wasn't even fresh: I did it twenty-five days into a month of playing at least eight hours a day.

It heated up outside again, and I spent the final day of the challenge slogging through heat exhaustion once more, which brutally bookended the challenge. I struggled to sleep at night. My office hit ninety degrees, and I couldn't focus on the cards. Math slipped away, but I completed my challenge with three hours to spare. And at the end, looking back, I know that I stood on top of that mountain and felt that breeze, and that thousands of people tuned in to see me do it. F2K felt like a distant memory, and the things I still cared about were now earning their places in my brain because they were important to me, rather than because someone else had manipulatively placed them there.

It's impossible to feel certain that I'm doing something good. I don't trust myself enough. Maybe I'm just hiding in a game of canasta. I've managed to find an environment where I can play games without my grandfather's mental illness distracting me, and viewers pay my bills. Maybe I'm in a cult and don't realize it, or maybe I'm legitimizing an industry which should be burned to the ground. Maybe I'm enabling cruelty and discrimination which don't have any right to exist on our planet. But I'm doing something, and people like it, and I'm good at it. I'm really good.

CATS

I'm not sure I'll ever function well in relationships again. Maybe nobody does, and that's actually pretty normal. I don't know. Whatever I had with my partner ended in the second year of the pandemic, as our dual anxieties played off each other in increasingly negative ways.

One day we got into an argument about whether I was trying hard enough to remember to give my cats medication. I was, as a general rule, failing to keep up with chores and responsibilities. The argument continued into my workday, and when I took a break to get a glass of water, she confronted me about it again in our kitchen. I tried to deflect her and went back into my studio, but she followed me in, and tried to argue with me while I was live to thousands of people, holding the mute button on my microphone and trying desperately to tell her that this wasn't okay, that it was stretching the most vulnerable fibers of my heart until I felt them all snap. After that, I couldn't function with her in the apartment with me anymore. We separated for a few months, and the next time we talked in person I had a panic attack when she stood up. I decided I wasn't going to try to make it work anymore, after that.

I don't have anything bad to say about her. In other breakups, my partners have guilted me and made me feel like I'm to blame, or stolen my cats. She didn't do any of that. She cried a lot and told me how sorry she was and made me lists of accounts that I would need to change. I gave her enough money to cover the rest of her degree. We don't hate each other; we just didn't work out.

After that, my cats and I were alone in the apartment. We laid in the sun on the floor together, and played with their toys. I slowly reorganized the living area to be able to have guests—an activity which left me with fitful nightmares after every visitor as I struggled to let even close friends into my personal space. At night, I cuddled in bed with the cats.

Zephyr is named for the Ancient Greek god of the West Wind. He has a beautiful gray coat, with tinges of blue. I had adopted him when he was still tiny, playing with him for hours the day that I brought him home. When I got tired, I had laid down on the bed to take a nap, and he'd climbed up onto it and then sat on my chest, looking at my face and waiting for me to wake up and play more.

He trusts me completely. If he gets hurt, he hides under my legs. When we move to new places, I carry him around on my shoulder and let him sniff and explore all the cupboards and high shelves. If I stay up past our regular bedtime, he sits on my desk, just far enough away to give me space to work, and his eyes slowly close as he struggles to stay awake. Once I'm finally ready to sleep he jumps onto the bed and sits next to my pillow, patiently waiting for me to get under the covers and then lift them up so he can snuggle against my belly, where he'll stay until it starts to get too hot, at which point he gently—so he won't wake me if I'm already asleep—slinks up toward my pillow and settles with his head on my arm, outside the covers. Zephyr represents, shall we say, secure attachment. Confidence, love.

Xenia is named for the Ancient Greek cultural practice of guest-host relationships. My abusive ex found her on one of the busier parts of Laurel Canyon Boulevard, in Los Angeles. She was in the gutter, too small and weak to climb out of it as six lanes of traffic blazed past her, cars going wherever it was that their drivers mistakenly thought was more important. She was feral, flea-ridden, and malnourished, and had an upper-respiratory infection which was swelling her left eye shut—it has never fully recovered.

We took her in, and she was terrified of us. I lifted my knees up in bed, and she hid under them, presumably not aware that I still knew she was there. We kept her isolated in the bedroom for a few days while we treated her fleas and had the vet run tests on her to make sure she didn't have anything contagious.

After a day or so she noticed that there was another cat in the apartment, and sat on the inside of the bedroom door, meowing for Zephyr to rescue her. And he did, as much as he could; he sat at the other side of the door and pawed at her underneath it. When we finally opened the door, she ran at him so energetically that he shied away, and she chased him until he'd had enough time to realize that she wasn't a threat; she was a kitten small enough to fit in the front pocket of one of my hoodies who was convinced she'd just found her mother again. Zephyr rose to the occasion, and they have been inseparable ever since. Xenia perhaps represents anxiety, or alertness. Or the ever-present sense of danger. Before she was strong enough to run away from me, I used to carry her around on my shoulder and sing to her.

Xenia still isn't as comfortable with me as Zephyr, but after I'd fed and protected her for five years or so she started sleeping next to my feet. After another two years she was behind my knees, then the next winter she was against my belly—causing Zephyr some discomfort as she basically tried to lie directly on top of where he was under the blankets.

Nowadays she'll come and check in with me before she settles down. She walks up to the top of the covers and asks me to lift them up. She sniffs at my hand, and makes little meowing sounds at Zephyr. Sometimes they have bath time. Two times she's actually gotten completely under the blankets and settled down against my arm or my chest. Most of the time she's more comfortable saying goodnight, then wandering back down to the middle of the bed and flopping down against whatever part of my body provides the appropriate amount of warmth that night.

I used to relate to Zephyr much more, but after a few years of streaming, a pandemic, some wars, and a good amount of behavioral engineering targeted at me by billion-dollar tech companies, I've started to come around to Xenia's point of view.

It's easy to feel dumb when I am trying to wind down from a stressful day blazing trails on the Internet frontier, and I've been procrastinating on going to bed for two hours because my brain is stuck in a loop about something which is happening in another city or country, or about something someone I don't even care about said of me—and then I finally climb into bed and almost immediately have two cats sandwiching me, bathing and sleeping and twitching in their dreams. What, exactly, were my concerns about? How had I thought they were more important than this? While my logical mind insists that the goings-on of the world at large have significance, there are tens of thousands of years of evolution which disagree and tell me that the two warm mammals who love me are the only thing in the entire world.

What if we all just loved the things close to us? How hard would it be to just not send that negative message, or abuse that stranger? I suppose, logically, that it must be very hard. But emotionally, while my cats cleanse all the negativity out of my body, I can't say that that makes any sense.

***

In June 2022, almost a year to the day after I found out John had stopped paying me for my work at F2K, I made my first ever offer on a house. I had been looking for one in the Seattle area for almost six months, and finally found one that was perfect for me. The next day I heard that my offer had been accepted. Two weeks later I was turning the key to open the door into a space filled with new possibilities, much larger than the tiny apartment which I had shared with another person through the first two years of the pandemic. Instead of having just my studio to work in and my bed to sleep, I could have so much more! I decided one of the rooms would be a guest room.

The first person I had come to stay was Hannah, who visited for a week in July. I kept the cats out of the guest room because she's allergic,[69] and just barely managed to get it set up properly before she arrived. She had to make do without curtains, but the windows were quite private, and she didn't complain. It was the first time we'd met in person in three-and-a-half years of working together, and she was all of the beautiful things I knew that she'd be and more.

She spent the first day of her visit cooking me food, delicious Korean barbecue, and I remembered John telling me about how he wanted us to all live on the same street so he could barbecue food for us. It was not lost on me that Hannah was the person who was actually in my house doing that for me.

We talked, sometimes for the entire day nonstop. If we needed to go to the store, we would talk for thirty minutes in the living room, then one of us would say "well we'd better get going," and then we'd talk for thirty minutes by the front door, until one of us said "okay, let's go before they shut." Then we'd talk nonstop in the car, and walking to the store, and on the way back, and while we unloaded what we'd bought.

I set her up so she could play *World of Warcraft* with her friends in my second office, and let her use my main streaming computer to do it until I'd worked out a way for that to be comfortable for her. She was amazed at my three 32" monitors, stream deck, audio interface, tablet I could write on with a stylus, professional

---

69   Hannah decided she wasn't allergic enough to deny herself cat cuddles, and I'm pretty sure Zephyr liked her more than he liked me by the end of the week.

microphone, sit/stand desk, integrated RGB background lights, and dSLR camera, and said she'd never seen a "real" streaming setup before. She'd made partner on Twitch while she'd been working with her Axie Guild, but she'd done it without anywhere near the number of gadgets I had.

I decided I wanted her to see more, so I got in touch with a friend and managed to get us a tour of the Evil Geniuses esports team's offices in Seattle. She wandered through the massive space, seeing all the desks and shared workspaces, the kitchen with snacks and food, streaming rooms, conference rooms, and gorgeous view of the Puget Sound, and I reflected on how everything she'd done, she'd done sitting on her own in a tiny house in inner city St. Louis, where she could hear gunshots most nights.

In the same way that my cats snap me back to reality, being in an actual physical space with Hannah made everything about her tangible and real. I hope to live in this house for decades, but for me, my living room will always be the room where she broke down and told me—through tears—that she had been working in content creation for seven years and felt like no one had ever listened to her.

***

Sometimes readers wonder if this is a love story—which is fair, because it is. But they get confused about what that means. Hannah and I love each other deeply and ferociously. If you cross either of us, you will answer to the other. You can be forgiven, to some extent, for thinking that that means we should have some sort of Disney romance for your narrative satisfaction—and our own. It would be nice if Disney romances were real.

But, in the real world, loving someone does not mean you are suddenly a prince and princess together. I am an abuse victim, and my relationship with my own sexuality is difficult on my own, let alone if someone else gets involved. When I felt like I was starting to feel whole again after my abusive relationship, I went and stayed with a friend for a weekend and got sexually assaulted by her roommate. To say that that set me back would be a massive understatement. I have panic attacks thinking about sex and relationships. Since breaking up with my last partner, I've slowly been processing the idea that I might never have one again, and trying to work out how I could commit to loving someone when I know that a single argument could leave me struggling to breathe, sitting on the floor of the bathroom with my knees hugged against my chest and the door locked.

And Hannah is an abuse victim, too. Actively! The idea of connecting deeply and romantically with someone in the streaming space is not appealing to a person who has been hurt and abused by that space for much of her adult life, and who is *currently* being harassed by an ex within it. And she's an entire whole person alongside that, too, full of intricacies and experiences which are hers to keep to herself.

Maybe somewhere out there, there's a port with a quiet beach, fiber internet, and an H Mart, and Hannah and I will someday find it and be happy. Maybe we'll each find someone else to be with, and be happy with them, and all of us will live on the same street. But it's hard for either of us to imagine any of that right now, because right now we are struggling for breath as she tries to keep me angled into the waves of the storm.

***

Streaming is a gigantic, multi-faceted, complicated industry. It's the new face of entertainment for an online generation who demand engagement and attention. The ways in which it is monetized, exploitative, dangerous, and enlightening are even more complex. When something is far too complex to properly understand, we have to come up with simple models to allow us to function, but we're looking at something which none of our instincts are equipped to handle. We think that the ping on our phone is something important to our lives—an alarm or a request from a friend—but instead, it's a company trying to sell us something. We think that the beautiful human who is talking to us and saying our name cares about us, but really they are at work, and we are one of hundreds or thousands of faceless consumers of their content whom they have little real connection to.

And everything that goes on behind the scenes is even more bizarre. Broken people invent broken solutions to problems created for them by a broken world. Sexism, objectification, exploitation, wealth inequality, a lack of social support programs and a breakdown of neighborhood communities and friend groups leave them fighting it all on their own, sometimes even isolated inside during a pandemic.

There are two very important steps that I take when I am faced with something that I don't understand.

First, I accept that I don't understand it, and give it the benefit of the doubt. I start experimenting with what happens when I try to make it do what I hope it can achieve. If I stream, what happens? If I try to make friendships with streamers, what happens? If I treat people with respect, what happens? If I trust people, what happens?

Many humans will betray you, given the right circumstances, but discovering that those circumstances exist doesn't mean you have to lose all trust in humanity—instead, your increased understanding of those circumstances could help you to avoid them in the future, and it might even strengthen your trust in humanity when you see that those circumstances aren't present.

I will never know everything about streaming, or family, or food, or anything else of complex consequence in the world.

It's all too deep and strange and connected. But every time I try something new and understand what happened and guess at why it did, I get a little bit closer to the truth, and when I take actions because of what I believe the truth is—not just what will get me attention, or satisfy my taste buds—I slowly get better and better at navigating all of these things.

The other step is to ask if I can skip understanding it altogether. If a friend has a car and is hungry for hangover food, I don't need to understand the inner workings of the car to trust that my friend can drive it to find us a burrito. Cryptocurrency and streaming teams and multimedia web conglomerates are incredibly complex, but often I can see that they're being run by someone who is greedy and self-interested, and I can simplify everything about them down to a belief that the person in charge, perhaps leveraged by the people providing the investment capital, will drive them wherever they want in order to get whatever they would like. If that's the direction I want to go, then I might hitch a ride; otherwise, I'd rather keep walking in the direction I'm going, thanks.

***

The Internet is a frontier for humanity—one where the resources we seek to secure and exploit for ourselves are the minds of other humans. Five generations ago, my ancestors moved to New Zealand, one of the last physical frontiers for European settlers. They had awkward and self-serving and violent and awful interactions with the Maori people there. They hunted some species of animals to extinction, and killed others with cats and other predators which they introduced, sometimes accidentally. They began a several-century-long process of turning an environment full of possibility into a country incredibly similar to the one which they had come from. A few things are different, here and there, but not all that many, considering.

When I look at a photo of my great-grandfather, I see my own smile, and when demons stir in my head, I remember that phone call with my grandfather in which he told me he was sending a message with his mind. I can't help but wonder if the ways in which I tackle this new frontier are ways passed down from the last of so many European generations who set off around the world. They learned that community was temporary and that they could sail so far away that they would never see their neighbors again in their lives. Until very recently, I sat in an apartment in a world where I barely knew my neighbors' names and they were a rotating cast of tenants in a building where I'd been paying more and more rent every year.

They learned that the resources available in the world were abundant—so many that they could not exhaust them in their entire lifetimes or even the lives of their children—and now I sit here in a world where we continue to treat resources as though they will never run out, even though some of them have, or are about to, or shouldn't ever be used or possessed by us in the first place.

They learned that other cultures were different from theirs and lied to themselves that those other cultures were inferior, and now I live in a world where so many of us still tell that lie.

Did my great-great-grandfather find a close friend who knew more than him and whom he knew he could trust? Did he build a little community that was about the things that were important to him? Did he scowl as investors tried to manipulate him and his friends into behaviors which would bring the investors profit at the cost of what their communities stood for? Did he fall in love, or pledge himself to a team, and make dumb decisions as a result when the people around him didn't treat him well? Did he feel lost and afraid—or is that a temporary confusion placed on just my generation by the companies pulling at my brain with their notifications and market strategies to control my behavior and make themselves money from my actions?

The likes on a recent tweet of mine cascade upwards on my other monitor, constantly reminding me that people like me, constantly reminding me that the next time I need reassurance that I am worthwhile, Twitter will be there waiting for me to share another interesting thought to keep people engaged on their platform.

I wonder, most of all, what we're going to make this new frontier look like. I see strong forces at work. Businesses want to make it a market, and have some success. But I see others at play, too. There are criminals who want to find the loopholes which can hurt people. There are lovers who want to find partners, and artists who want to make art, and socialites who want to find friends. I see us finding every way to consume human attention, and wonder what will be left to exploit once it is all gone. What changes will the frontier make to us? We cannot shape it without it shaping us back. How will we be different in another ten years? Will I have contributed a small step toward shaping this frontier to bring us happiness and kindness? Toward empowering those with potential whom others won't allow to contribute?

One of the most difficult long-term pressures in streaming is that you begin to lose who you are. You put all of yourself into your content, but as you make it, people watch it and decide what it is for themselves.

I didn't ever intend to be a comfortable voice for falling asleep to, but for many people, that is my use, and so now that is one of the things I am. All of a sudden, I feel bad about making loud noises when I stream because I realize that I might be waking up people who'd trusted me to play in the background while they fell asleep.

I don't try to be better than other people, but sometimes people will make lists of who the best *Slay the Spire* players are and put me at the top of them, and all of a sudden, my effect on others is that I'm an attack on their ego and worth, even though I never asked or planned or tried to be that thing.

It's important for me to sit down and find myself again, every now and then. Work out which parts of the story about my life and the things that I do are the parts that I personally think are me. If you don't like who I am . . . well, I'm not sure how you made it this far, but I hope you'll still feel free to fall asleep to my voice or use my content for whatever it offers you. And if you do like who I am, now you know a lot more of the full story.

EPILOGUE

The most beautiful thing about games is that they have the ability to treat us equally. If I were to play *Hearthstone*, I'd be treated with more kindness and support than Pathra was, even though she was competing at the highest level and I would be a complete beginner, just because I am a guy. Other men would look at me and say "You can tell he's good, because of how he talks about the game." They would forgive my losses and mistakes—"he's only human"—and emphasize my successes—"you can see how quickly he's improving!" *Hearthstone* itself doesn't care about that, though. If I played games against Pathra, she would destroy me, over and over again, and *Hearthstone* would give the world its unbiased feedback that she was impressive and worthy, and I was the one who was not able to compete.

This lends them well to communicating about the world, because they allow us to begin with a common ground. I can ask a question about the game, and the question will mean the same thing to everyone who plays that game. And if I answer it, the answer I find will make sense for everyone. The game doesn't ask what gender you are, or where you grew up, or if you look nice, before it decides how to treat you.

This doesn't work for most things in life. When I write about my personality and experience away from games, I understand that it can't ever make sense to everyone else. The world doesn't treat me the same way it treats you.

In some ways, it favors me. I enjoy many privileges as a white man which most readers will have already heard about or even experienced themselves. And I enjoy many other, more specific favors from the world. I have a fairly average-shaped male body, so it is easy for me to shop for clothes and fit in spaces. I have blue eyes, and sometimes people fall into them. I was born to hardworking parents who sent me to good schools, and my mother's parents lived four houses up the street (and then moved in next door so they could be closer) and supported me and were kind to me and loved me. I know how to do the things which "smart" people are meant to be able to do, and I know what it's like to be loved and to love others. I have never gone hungry for want of money to buy food.

In others, it scorns me. Some of them are silly inconveniences—I am left-handed, and so I hate scissors. Others are more serious. I have some predilection for abusive relationships, perhaps because I trust others and don't turn away from them as quickly as I should. I have a couple of chronic genetic diseases lurking in me: psoriasis, that makes my skin uncomfortable and sometimes ugly; and bipolar disorder, which I always worry will boil up from somewhere deep within my brain and send me on a journey out of my own reality. I moved away from my entire extended family when I was twelve, and I have longed, but failed, to put those pieces back together and have a family again ever since. We moved to a new country which was strange and sometimes cruel, and I have been treated strangely and sometimes cruelly by people who find me unusual.

The best metaphor I ever heard about being an immigrant was about plants. Plants have complex root systems to pull nutrition from the soil, and their most important root is called their "taproot." It grows vertically downward, searching for water held deep in the soil. When plants are transplanted, their taproot may be lost, or inadequately preserved. It may never regrow. I don't have a taproot—it got lost when I was 12. When people talk to me about their heritage in the United States, I'm unable to relate. When they feel confident because their families have been enduring hardships here for generations, I feel insecure because mine has not. I don't know who to turn to for help in this country; none of my connections here go back more than twenty years.

So, when I ask questions in a book about life, I know that they don't all mean the same things to me as they do to you. And when I try to answer them, even if I get an answer for myself, I don't know if it would make sense for you. Maybe you could send me one of your answers. I have fragments of my own. I know that we should care about each other. I know that it doesn't matter whether or not the world is a cruel place when I am choosing whether to be cruel or kind—every kindness that I put out into the world counts, and it often counts more than I realize. I know that that's true—that even if the world ends thirty years from now, all that kindness will still have been worth it. Dying at the end makes the journey more important, not less.

I know that I need to make enough to get by and that I probably shouldn't try to make very much more than that, and that if I find that I am making more than I need, I can enrich my life and the lives of others by spending time on charity projects. I know that trying to maximize how many friends I make, people I inspire, shoes I walk in, or problems I solve is a lot more fun than maximizing how much money I make. I know that some other people don't realize this, and will try to make money off me, and that, a lot of the time for a lot of those people, I can simply tell them to go fuck themselves.

I know that strategy games are hard and I also know that they're all sort of the same game, and that investment is that game, and management is that game, and abuse is that game, and maybe life is that game, and that I can choose how hard I try to win and how hard I try to make the game fun for everyone involved. I can choose whether I want to manipulate and outmaneuver people to beat them or encourage and applaud people so they'll want to keep playing with me. I can choose to build an entirely new game that people will like to play, and that will put good out into the world.

I know that we could at least double the good in the world by just treating people who aren't men better, that wanting to have sex with someone isn't the only thing that a relationship can be about, and that you probably shouldn't give your kids an iPhone or let them on social media, but I don't really know what you're meant to give your kids instead.

I know that every tiny improvement I make can make a gigantic change in the world, especially if I make it a habit and keep doing it every day.

I know that this isn't a story about particularly bad people, but a story about people like me who had a couple of things go differently in their lives which led to them being on their end of the call instead of mine. And it's a story about how I'm a bad person sometimes, too. Being a bad person once doesn't mean I can't spend today and tomorrow trying to be a good one. And the next day and the day after that.

And it's a story about Hannah. We're all lumps of coal, and it's largely out of our control what happens to us, but when you meet a diamond, my opinion is that you should shut up and listen to her and support her when she asks you to, in the ways that she wants.

ACKNOWLEDGEMENTS

I did not realize, upon starting this book, quite how difficult the undertaking was. Sitting in your room on your own and writing a book is no easy task. Fortunately, I have not been on my own.

Firstly, thank you Hannah, for your guidance, temperance, and trust. Without you this probably wouldn't have ever even managed to be a fully-fledged blog post. And to Jay, Anna, Stephanie, George, and Hannah N., for seeing this project and judging it worthy of tidying, editing, and publishing. To Zyalin for bringing my feelings alive with your cover art, and to Ray for giving your voice to my words.

Next, thank you to everyone from outside my world who has tried their hardest to understand the strange space I live in and support me in making sense of it. Mum, Dad, Dylan, Rob, Bert, Caitlin, May, Char, Martin, Yair, Mike, and the pages-long list of others who have entertained and reflected upon my stories at dinners, parties, game nights, in bars, on trips, and over the phone or Internet, or have offered me expertise and advice on journalistic ethics or cryptocurrency or whatever else I have found myself struggling to understand. I am surrounded by people who say "yes" when I ask for help, and I am eternally grateful for all of you.

To everyone who has sat and spoken with me about their own experiences, thank you for helping to forge and direct my thoughts, and for lending your own stories to this work. Some of you would rather not be named here, and I thank you for trusting me with your voices despite that.

For those I can name: thank you Filthy, Pathra, Nicholena, Emma, Risa, Gaby, Luis, Caleb, Cate, Nic, Wirtual, Sun, Serge, Audrey, Amy, Voxy, Nenko, Emily, Ramblinnn, Dylan, Scott, Peter, Yeti, Honk, Jen, Dan, Bloody, Edison, Sim, Lady, Kyle, Clara, Allie, Sasha, Alex, Baalor, Electrobolt, Jessica, Lex, Geoff, and so many others. There's no sensible way to draw a line where some people have been helpful and are worth thanking by name and others are not, please know that I have cherished every conversation and piece of encouragement I've received from other streamers, and that I appreciate all of you. Sometimes just reading your own thoughts in your blog or Twitter posts has helped me to feel grounded. It can be nice just to hear that someone else is feeling the same sorts of things that you're feeling.

Thanks to everyone who was kind to me at F2K, or who has been kind on Twitch, or at conventions and other events.

Thanks to my community; to everyone from the people who have stopped by and enjoyed my show once, to those of you who watch every YouTube video, or catch almost every livestream, and share fun and kind thoughts and pictures in our Discord.

And thanks to Zephyr, who has been through more shit with me at this point than any other living being, and to Xenia, who is a close second, and who still finds me terrifying, but increasingly seems to be able to tell when I could use a hug.

CPSIA information can be obtained
at www.ICGtesting.com
Printed in the USA
BVHW080817260423
663030BV00004B/8

9 781739 285906